降击神通

AVATAR

THE LAST AIRBENDER™

Created by
Bryan Konietzko
Michael Dante DiMartino

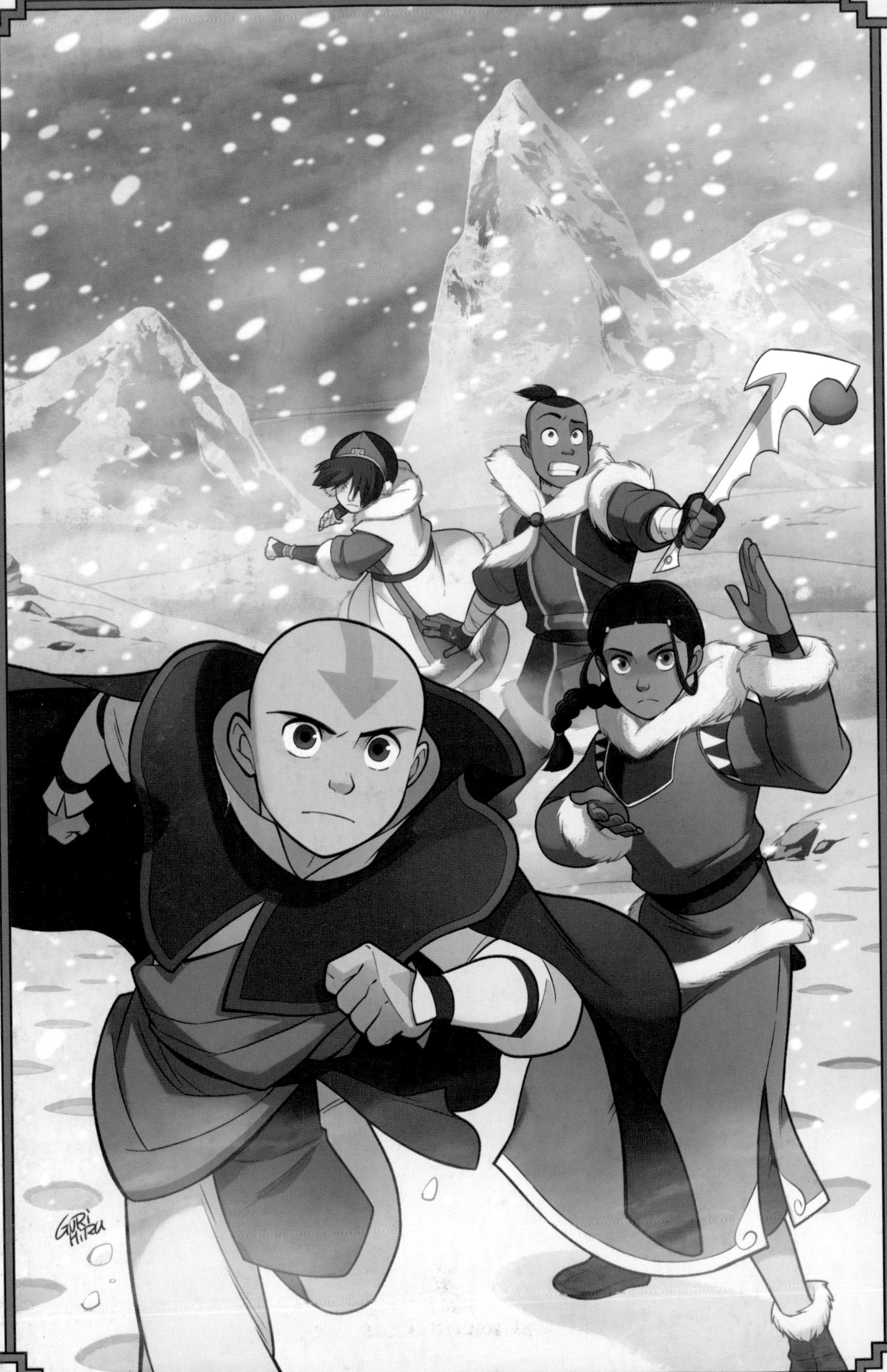
GURI HIRU

nickelodeon

降击神通

AVATAR

THE LAST AIRBENDER

NORTH AND SOUTH · PART THREE

script
GENE LUEN YANG

art and cover
GURIHIRU

lettering
MICHAEL HEISLER

DARK HORSE BOOKS

president and publisher
MIKE RICHARDSON

editor
DAVE MARSHALL

assistant editor
RACHEL ROBERTS

collection designer
SARAH TERRY

digital art technician
CHRISTIANNE GOUDREAU

Special thanks to Linda Lee, Kat van Dam, James Salerno, and Joan Hilty
at Nickelodeon, and to Bryan Konietzko and Michael Dante DiMartino.

Published by **Dark Horse Books**
A division of Dark Horse Comics, Inc.
10956 SE Main Street, Milwaukie, OR 97222

DarkHorse.com
Nick.com

International Licensing: (503) 905-2377
Comic Shop Locator Service: (888) 266-4226

First edition: April 2017 | ISBN 978-1-50670-130-1

1 3 5 7 9 10 8 6 4 2
Printed in China

PENGA! THE DARK ONE! GIVE ME A HAND HERE, WILL YOU?

SHOVE!

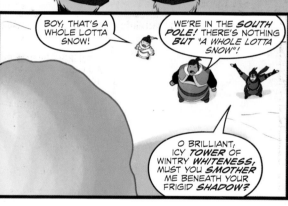

BOY, THAT'S A WHOLE LOTTA SNOW!

WE'RE IN THE SOUTH POLE! THERE'S NOTHING BUT "A WHOLE LOTTA SNOW"!

O BRILLIANT, ICY TOWER OF WINTRY WHITENESS, MUST YOU SMOTHER ME BENEATH YOUR FRIGID SHADOW?

NOW THAT WE'VE CLEARED THAT OUT OF THE WAY, WHY DON'T YOU GUYS HELP ME WITH --

K'REEAAK

RUMBLE!

AVALANCHE!

RUN FOR YOUR LIVES, METAL-BENDERS!

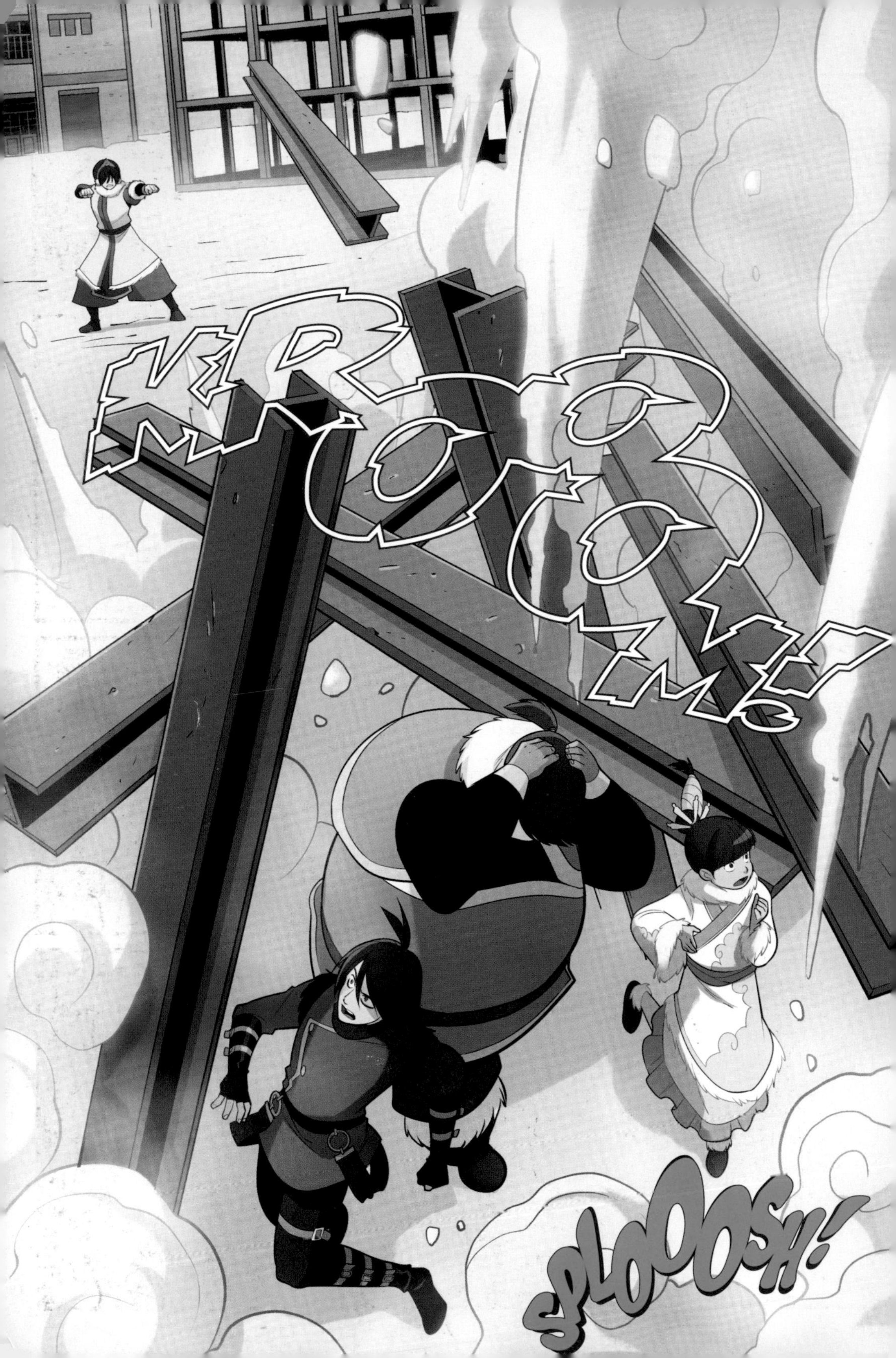
KROOOM!
SPLOOOSH!

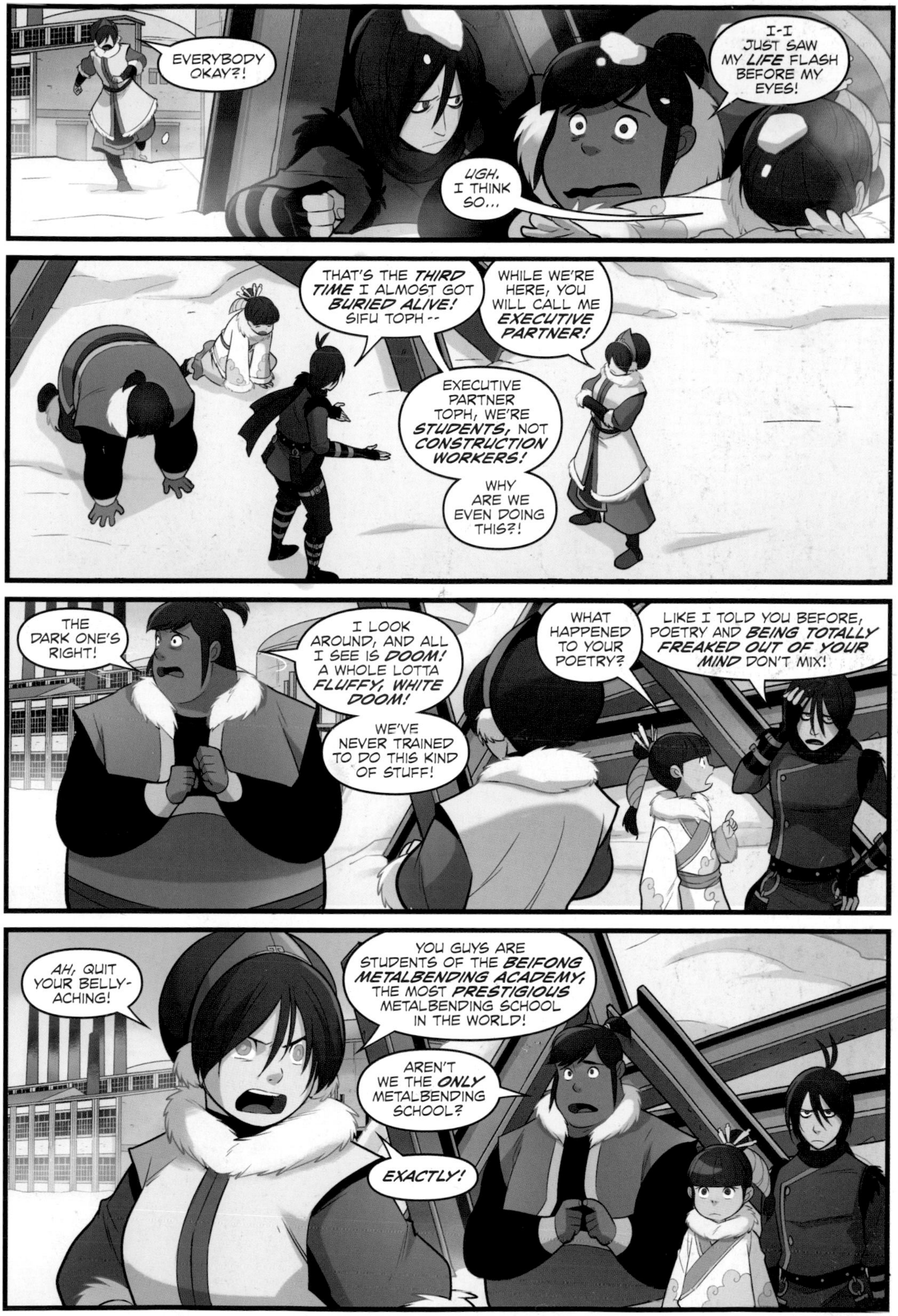
EVERYBODY OKAY?!
I-I JUST SAW MY *LIFE* FLASH BEFORE MY EYES!
UGH. I THINK SO...
THAT'S THE *THIRD TIME* I ALMOST GOT *BURIED ALIVE!* SIFU TOPH --
WHILE WE'RE HERE, YOU WILL CALL ME *EXECUTIVE PARTNER!*
EXECUTIVE PARTNER TOPH, WE'RE *STUDENTS,* NOT *CONSTRUCTION WORKERS!*
WHY ARE WE EVEN DOING THIS?!
THE DARK ONE'S RIGHT!
I LOOK AROUND, AND ALL I SEE IS *DOOM!* A WHOLE LOTTA *FLUFFY, WHITE DOOM!*
WE'VE NEVER TRAINED TO DO THIS KIND OF STUFF!
WHAT HAPPENED TO YOUR POETRY?
LIKE I TOLD YOU BEFORE, POETRY AND *BEING TOTALLY FREAKED OUT OF YOUR MIND* DON'T MIX!
AH, QUIT YOUR BELLY-ACHING!
YOU GUYS ARE STUDENTS OF THE *BEIFONG METALBENDING ACADEMY,* THE MOST *PRESTIGIOUS* METALBENDING SCHOOL IN THE WORLD!
AREN'T WE THE *ONLY* METALBENDING SCHOOL?
EXACTLY!

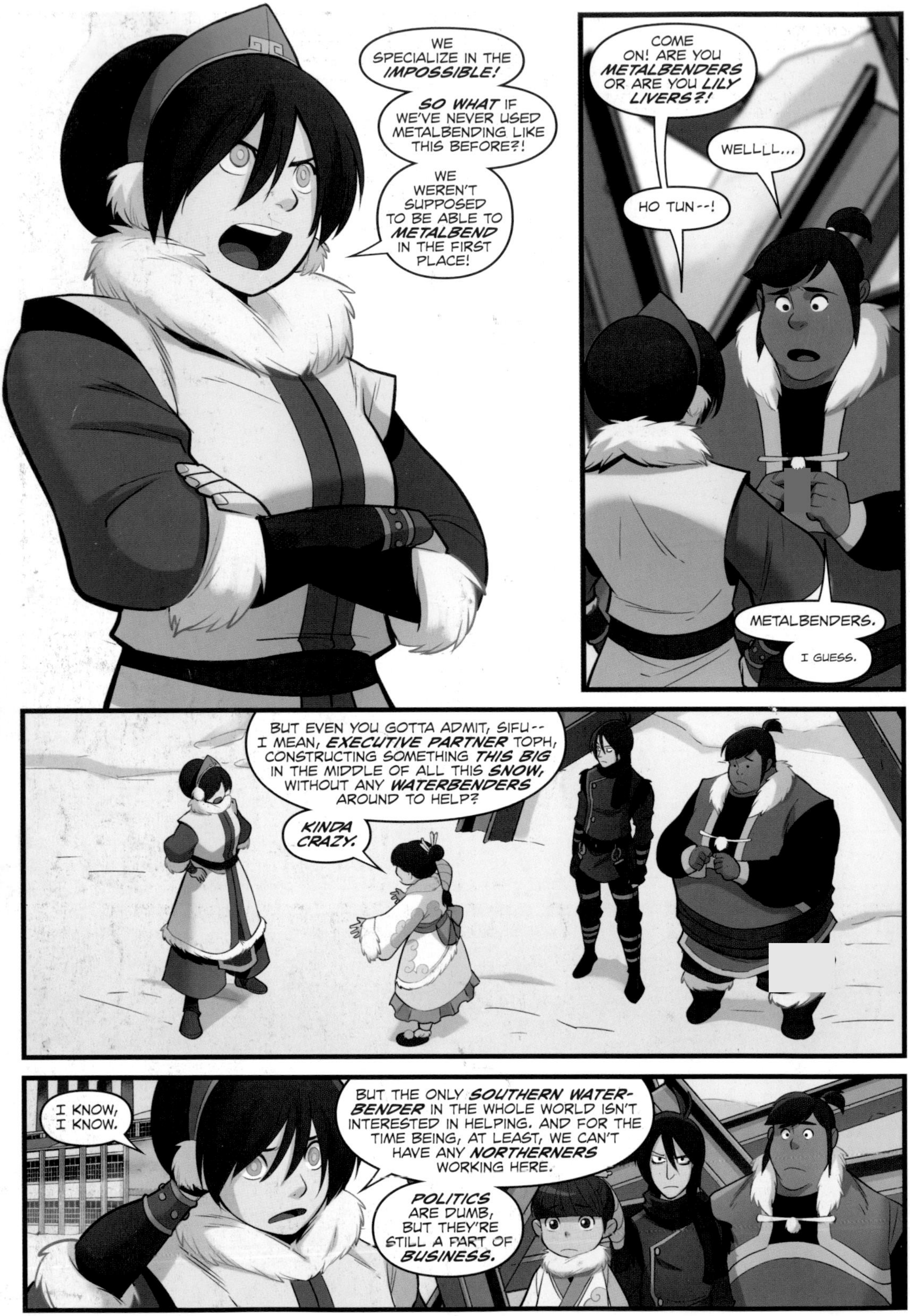

WE SPECIALIZE IN THE IMPOSSIBLE!
SO WHAT IF WE'VE NEVER USED METALBENDING LIKE THIS BEFORE?!
WE WEREN'T SUPPOSED TO BE ABLE TO METALBEND IN THE FIRST PLACE!
COME ON! ARE YOU METALBENDERS OR ARE YOU LILY LIVERS?!
HO TUN--!
WELLLL...
METALBENDERS.
I GUESS.
BUT EVEN YOU GOTTA ADMIT, SIFU-- I MEAN, EXECUTIVE PARTNER TOPH, CONSTRUCTING SOMETHING THIS BIG IN THE MIDDLE OF ALL THIS SNOW, WITHOUT ANY WATERBENDERS AROUND TO HELP?
KINDA CRAZY.
I KNOW, I KNOW.
BUT THE ONLY SOUTHERN WATER-BENDER IN THE WHOLE WORLD ISN'T INTERESTED IN HELPING. AND FOR THE TIME BEING, AT LEAST, WE CAN'T HAVE ANY NORTHERNERS WORKING HERE.
POLITICS ARE DUMB, BUT THEY'RE STILL A PART OF BUSINESS.

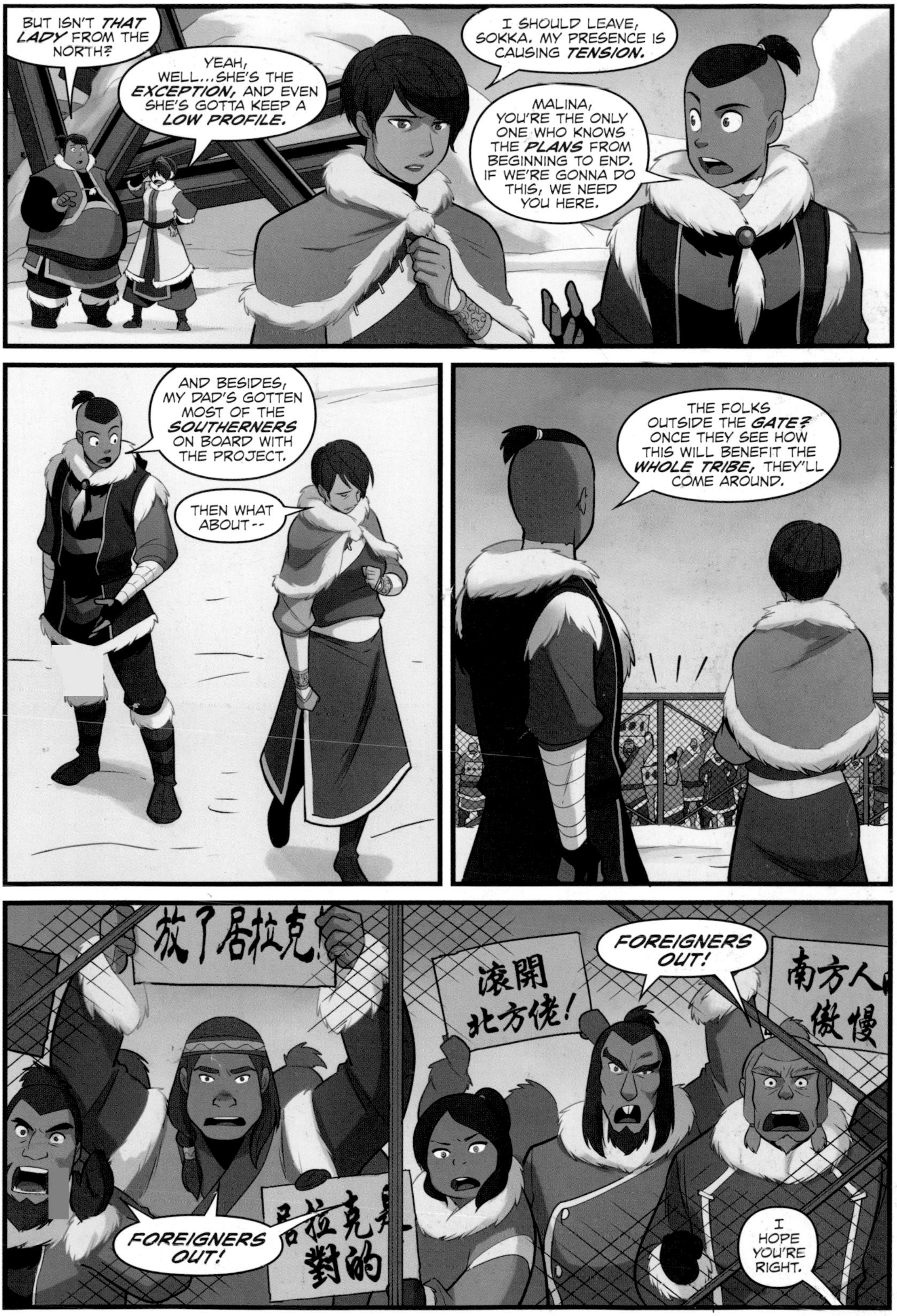
BUT ISN'T *THAT LADY* FROM THE NORTH?
YEAH, WELL...SHE'S THE *EXCEPTION,* AND EVEN SHE'S GOTTA KEEP A *LOW PROFILE.*
I SHOULD LEAVE, SOKKA. MY PRESENCE IS CAUSING *TENSION.*
MALINA, YOU'RE THE ONLY ONE WHO KNOWS THE *PLANS* FROM BEGINNING TO END. IF WE'RE GONNA DO THIS, WE NEED YOU HERE.
AND BESIDES, MY DAD'S GOTTEN MOST OF THE *SOUTHERNERS* ON BOARD WITH THE PROJECT.
THEN WHAT ABOUT--
THE FOLKS OUTSIDE THE *GATE?* ONCE THEY SEE HOW THIS WILL BENEFIT THE *WHOLE TRIBE,* THEY'LL COME AROUND.
放了居拉克
FOREIGNERS OUT!
對的
滾開
北方佬!
FOREIGNERS OUT!
傲慢
I HOPE YOU'RE RIGHT.

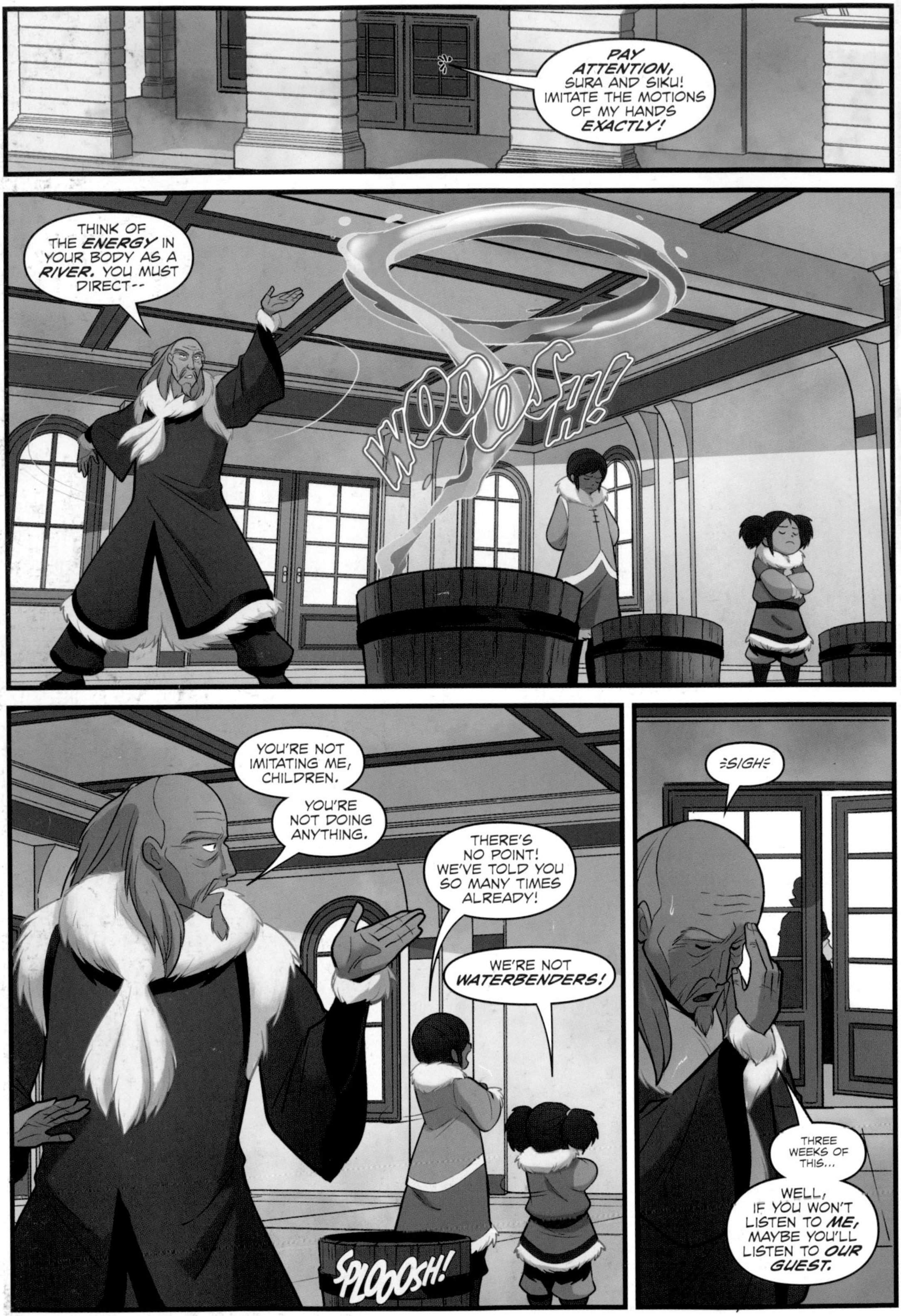
PAY ATTENTION, SURA AND SIKU! IMITATE THE MOTIONS OF MY HANDS EXACTLY!
THINK OF THE ENERGY IN YOUR BODY AS A RIVER. YOU MUST DIRECT--
WOOOOSH!
YOU'RE NOT IMITATING ME, CHILDREN.
YOU'RE NOT DOING ANYTHING.
THERE'S NO POINT! WE'VE TOLD YOU SO MANY TIMES ALREADY!
WE'RE NOT WATERBENDERS!
SPLOOOSH!
SIGH
THREE WEEKS OF THIS...
WELL, IF YOU WON'T LISTEN TO ME, MAYBE YOU'LL LISTEN TO OUR GUEST.

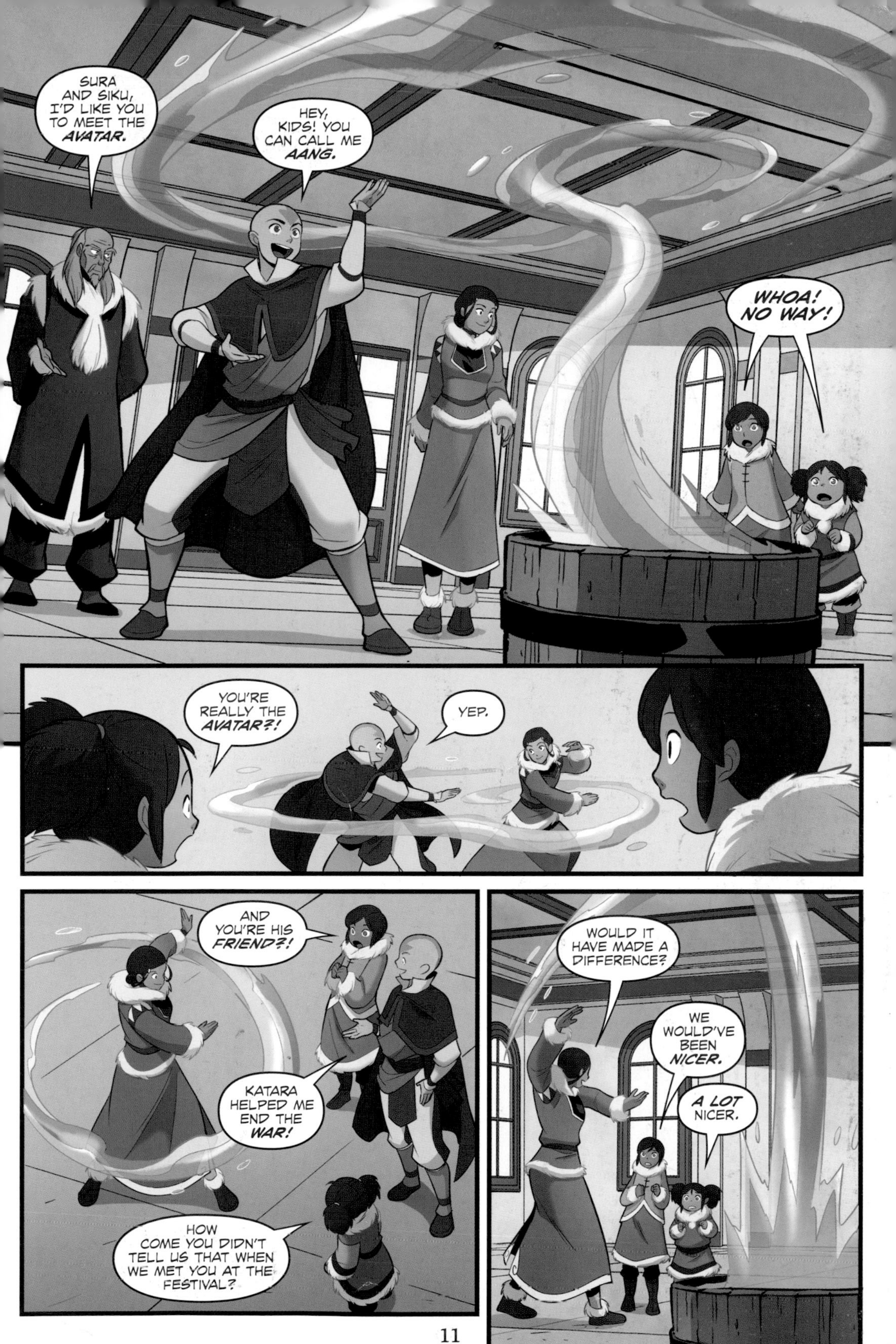
SURA AND SIKU, I'D LIKE YOU TO MEET THE AVATAR.
HEY, KIDS! YOU CAN CALL ME AANG.
WHOA! NO WAY!
YOU'RE REALLY THE AVATAR?!
YEP.
AND YOU'RE HIS FRIEND?!
KATARA HELPED ME END THE WAR!
HOW COME YOU DIDN'T TELL US THAT WHEN WE MET YOU AT THE FESTIVAL?
WOULD IT HAVE MADE A DIFFERENCE?
WE WOULD'VE BEEN NICER.
A LOT NICER.

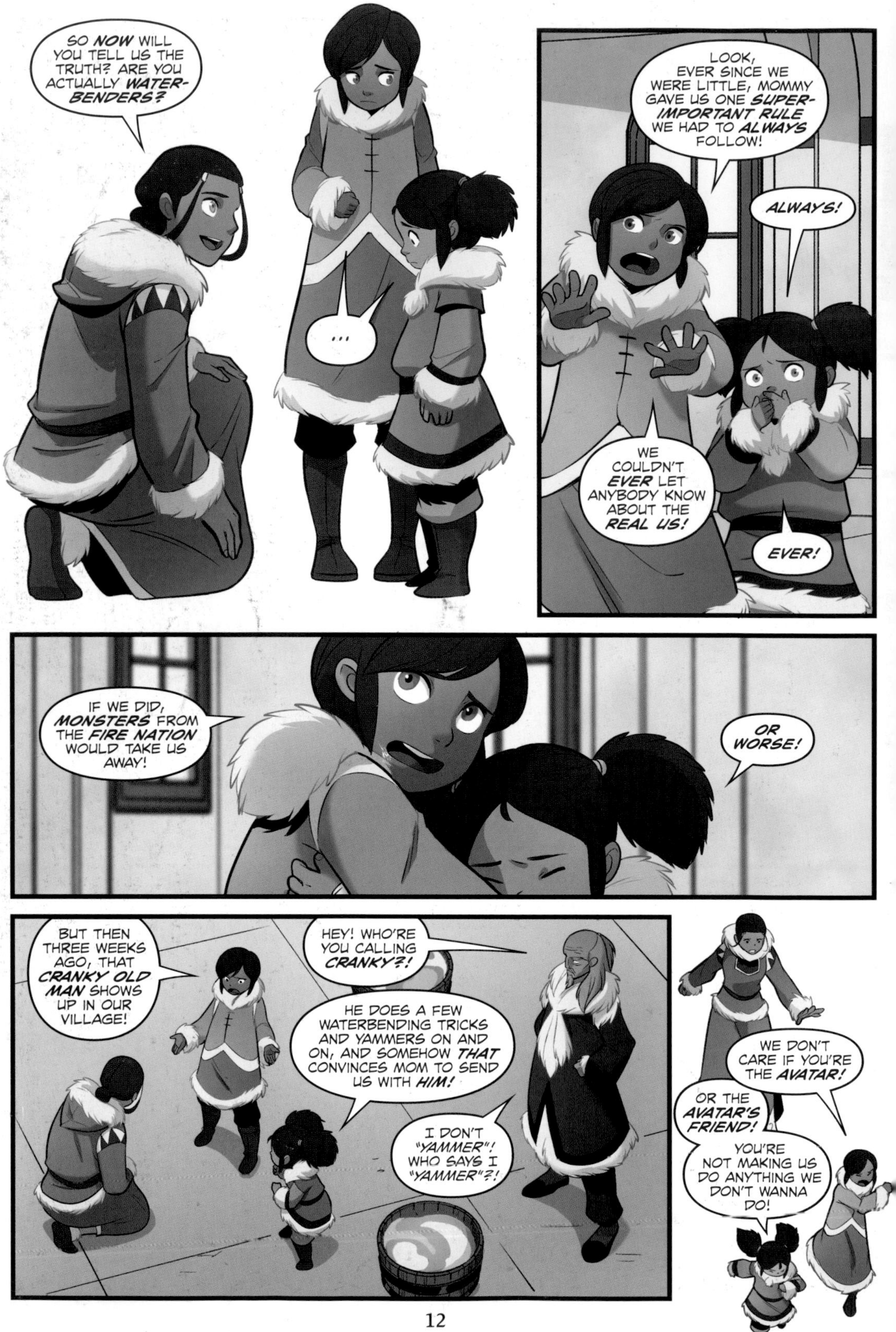
SO NOW WILL YOU TELL US THE TRUTH? ARE YOU ACTUALLY WATER-BENDERS?
...
LOOK, EVER SINCE WE WERE LITTLE, MOMMY GAVE US ONE SUPER-IMPORTANT RULE WE HAD TO ALWAYS FOLLOW!
ALWAYS!
WE COULDN'T EVER LET ANYBODY KNOW ABOUT THE REAL US!
EVER!
IF WE DID, MONSTERS FROM THE FIRE NATION WOULD TAKE US AWAY!
OR WORSE!
BUT THEN THREE WEEKS AGO, THAT CRANKY OLD MAN SHOWS UP IN OUR VILLAGE!
HEY! WHO'RE YOU CALLING CRANKY?!
HE DOES A FEW WATERBENDING TRICKS AND YAMMERS ON AND ON, AND SOMEHOW THAT CONVINCES MOM TO SEND US WITH HIM!
I DON'T "YAMMER"! WHO SAYS I "YAMMER"?!
WE DON'T CARE IF YOU'RE THE AVATAR!
OR THE AVATAR'S FRIEND!
YOU'RE NOT MAKING US DO ANYTHING WE DON'T WANNA DO!

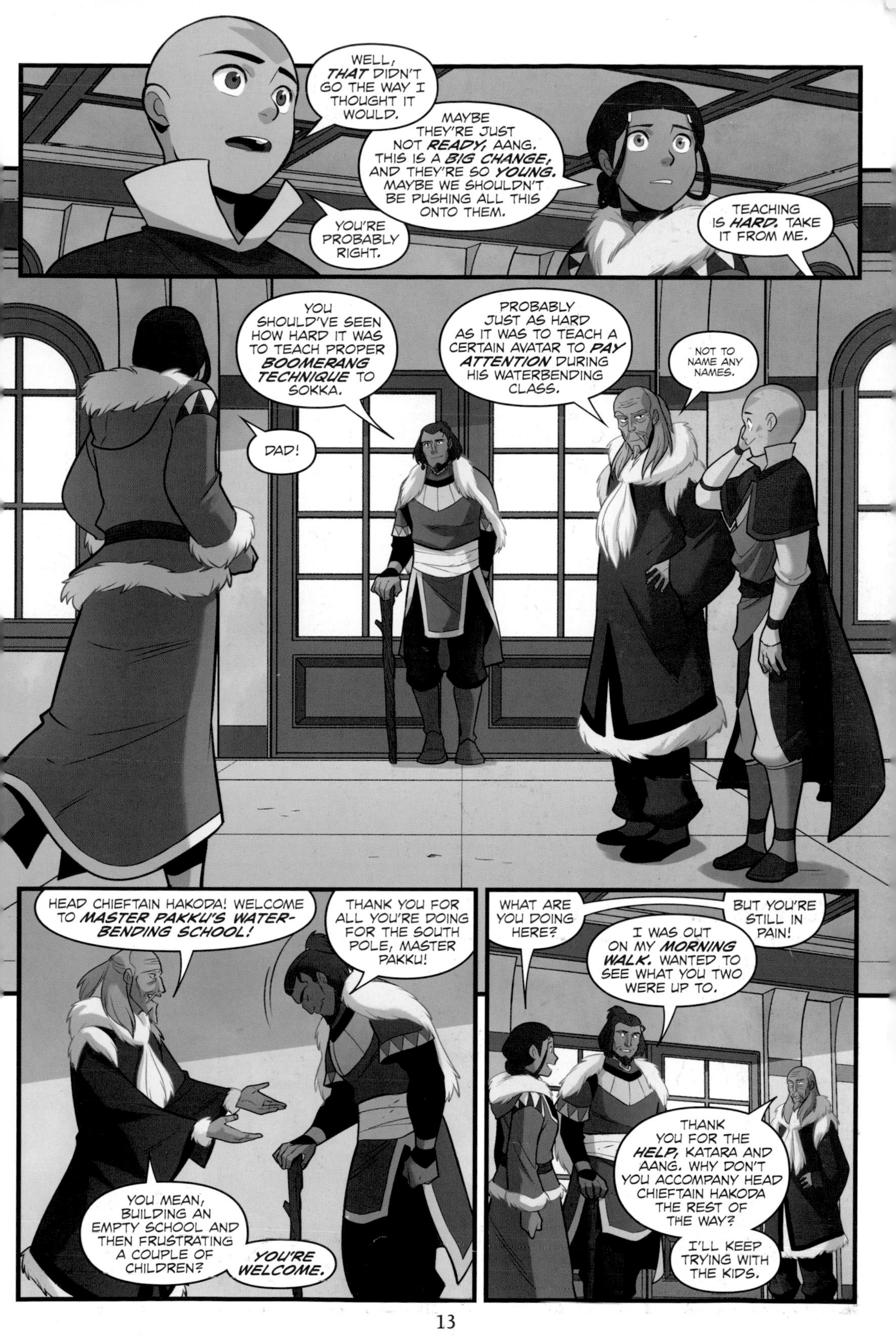
WELL, THAT DIDN'T GO THE WAY I THOUGHT IT WOULD.
MAYBE THEY'RE JUST NOT READY, AANG. THIS IS A BIG CHANGE, AND THEY'RE SO YOUNG. MAYBE WE SHOULDN'T BE PUSHING ALL THIS ONTO THEM.
YOU'RE PROBABLY RIGHT.
TEACHING IS HARD. TAKE IT FROM ME.
YOU SHOULD'VE SEEN HOW HARD IT WAS TO TEACH PROPER BOOMERANG TECHNIQUE TO SOKKA.
DAD!
PROBABLY JUST AS HARD AS IT WAS TO TEACH A CERTAIN AVATAR TO PAY ATTENTION DURING HIS WATERBENDING CLASS.
NOT TO NAME ANY NAMES.
HEAD CHIEFTAIN HAKODA! WELCOME TO MASTER PAKKU'S WATER-BENDING SCHOOL!
THANK YOU FOR ALL YOU'RE DOING FOR THE SOUTH POLE, MASTER PAKKU!
YOU MEAN, BUILDING AN EMPTY SCHOOL AND THEN FRUSTRATING A COUPLE OF CHILDREN?
YOU'RE WELCOME.
WHAT ARE YOU DOING HERE?
BUT YOU'RE STILL IN PAIN!
I WAS OUT ON MY MORNING WALK. WANTED TO SEE WHAT YOU TWO WERE UP TO.
THANK YOU FOR THE HELP, KATARA AND AANG. WHY DON'T YOU ACCOMPANY HEAD CHIEFTAIN HAKODA THE REST OF THE WAY?
I'LL KEEP TRYING WITH THE KIDS.

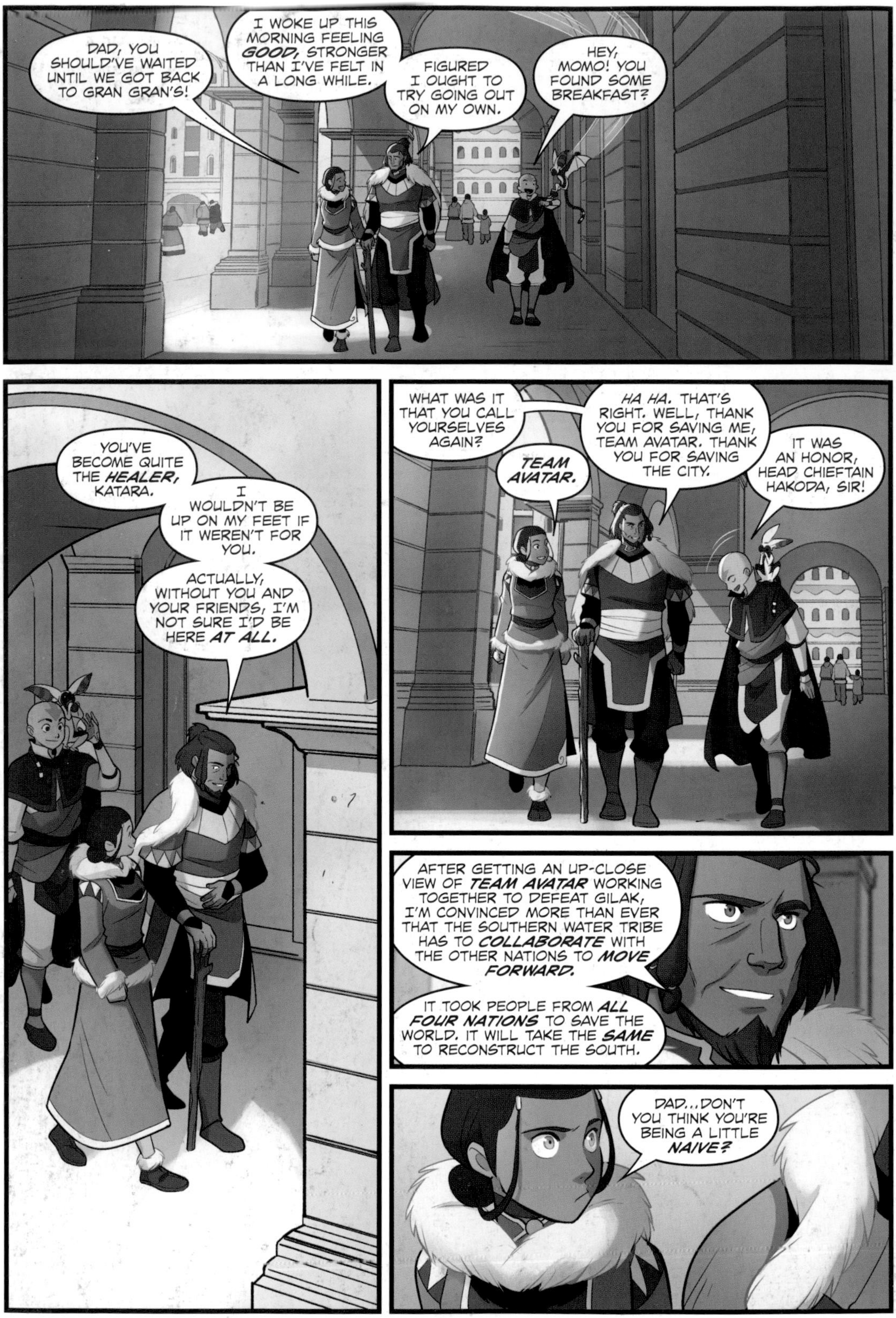
DAD, YOU SHOULD'VE WAITED UNTIL WE GOT BACK TO GRAN GRAN'S!
I WOKE UP THIS MORNING FEELING GOOD, STRONGER THAN I'VE FELT IN A LONG WHILE.
FIGURED I OUGHT TO TRY GOING OUT ON MY OWN.
HEY, MOMO! YOU FOUND SOME BREAKFAST?
YOU'VE BECOME QUITE THE HEALER, KATARA.
I WOULDN'T BE UP ON MY FEET IF IT WEREN'T FOR YOU.
ACTUALLY, WITHOUT YOU AND YOUR FRIENDS, I'M NOT SURE I'D BE HERE AT ALL.
WHAT WAS IT THAT YOU CALL YOURSELVES AGAIN?
TEAM AVATAR.
HA HA. THAT'S RIGHT. WELL, THANK YOU FOR SAVING ME, TEAM AVATAR. THANK YOU FOR SAVING THE CITY.
IT WAS AN HONOR, HEAD CHIEFTAIN HAKODA, SIR!
AFTER GETTING AN UP-CLOSE VIEW OF TEAM AVATAR WORKING TOGETHER TO DEFEAT GILAK, I'M CONVINCED MORE THAN EVER THAT THE SOUTHERN WATER TRIBE HAS TO COLLABORATE WITH THE OTHER NATIONS TO MOVE FORWARD.
IT TOOK PEOPLE FROM ALL FOUR NATIONS TO SAVE THE WORLD. IT WILL TAKE THE SAME TO RECONSTRUCT THE SOUTH.
DAD...DON'T YOU THINK YOU'RE BEING A LITTLE NAIVE?

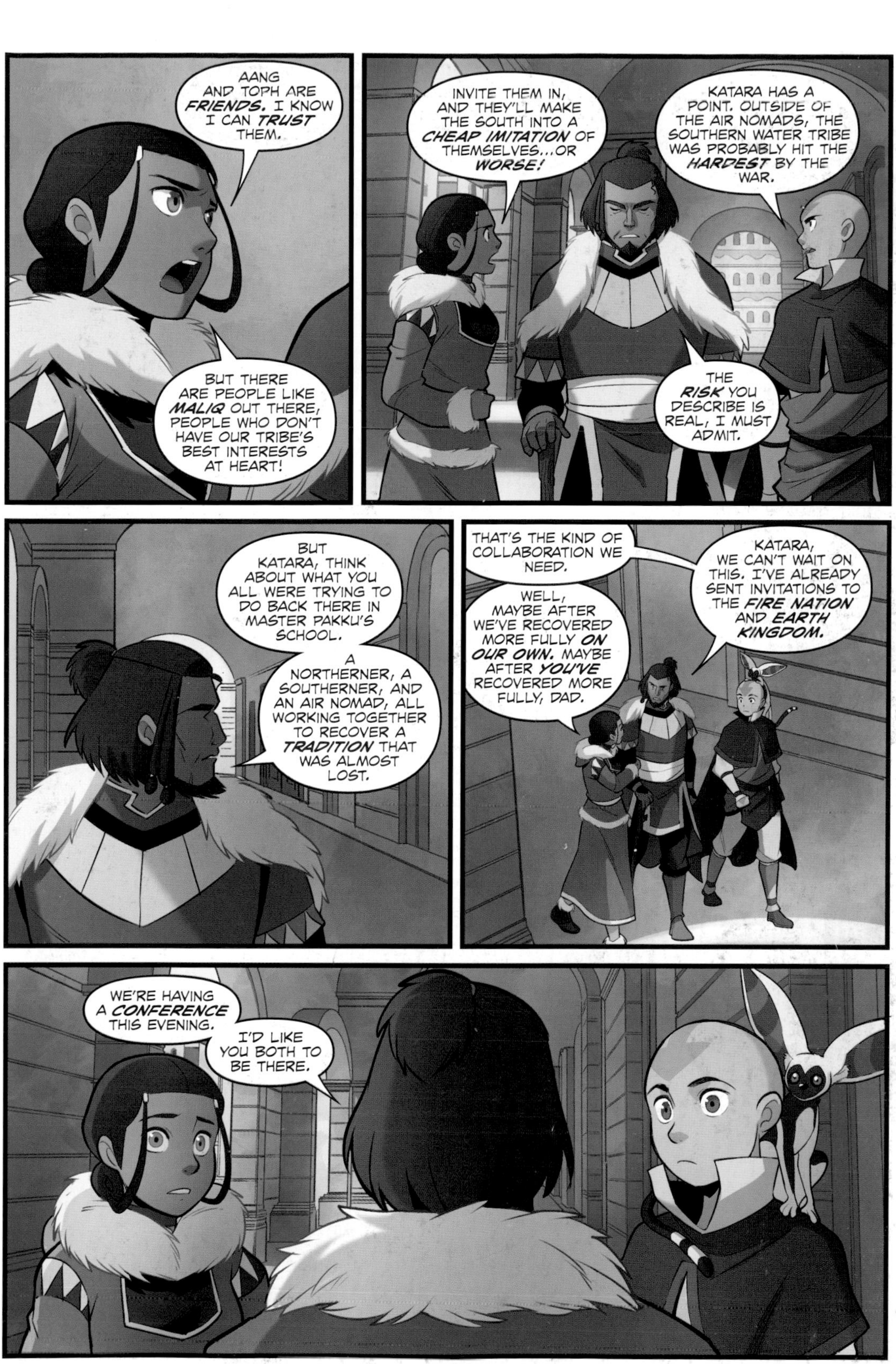
AANG AND TOPH ARE FRIENDS. I KNOW I CAN TRUST THEM.
BUT THERE ARE PEOPLE LIKE MALIQ OUT THERE, PEOPLE WHO DON'T HAVE OUR TRIBE'S BEST INTERESTS AT HEART!
INVITE THEM IN, AND THEY'LL MAKE THE SOUTH INTO A CHEAP IMITATION OF THEMSELVES...OR WORSE!
KATARA HAS A POINT. OUTSIDE OF THE AIR NOMADS, THE SOUTHERN WATER TRIBE WAS PROBABLY HIT THE HARDEST BY THE WAR.
THE RISK YOU DESCRIBE IS REAL, I MUST ADMIT.
BUT KATARA, THINK ABOUT WHAT YOU ALL WERE TRYING TO DO BACK THERE IN MASTER PAKKU'S SCHOOL.
A NORTHERNER, A SOUTHERNER, AND AN AIR NOMAD, ALL WORKING TOGETHER TO RECOVER A TRADITION THAT WAS ALMOST LOST.
THAT'S THE KIND OF COLLABORATION WE NEED.
WELL, MAYBE AFTER WE'VE RECOVERED MORE FULLY ON OUR OWN. MAYBE AFTER YOU'VE RECOVERED MORE FULLY, DAD.
KATARA, WE CAN'T WAIT ON THIS. I'VE ALREADY SENT INVITATIONS TO THE FIRE NATION AND EARTH KINGDOM.
WE'RE HAVING A CONFERENCE THIS EVENING.
I'D LIKE YOU BOTH TO BE THERE.

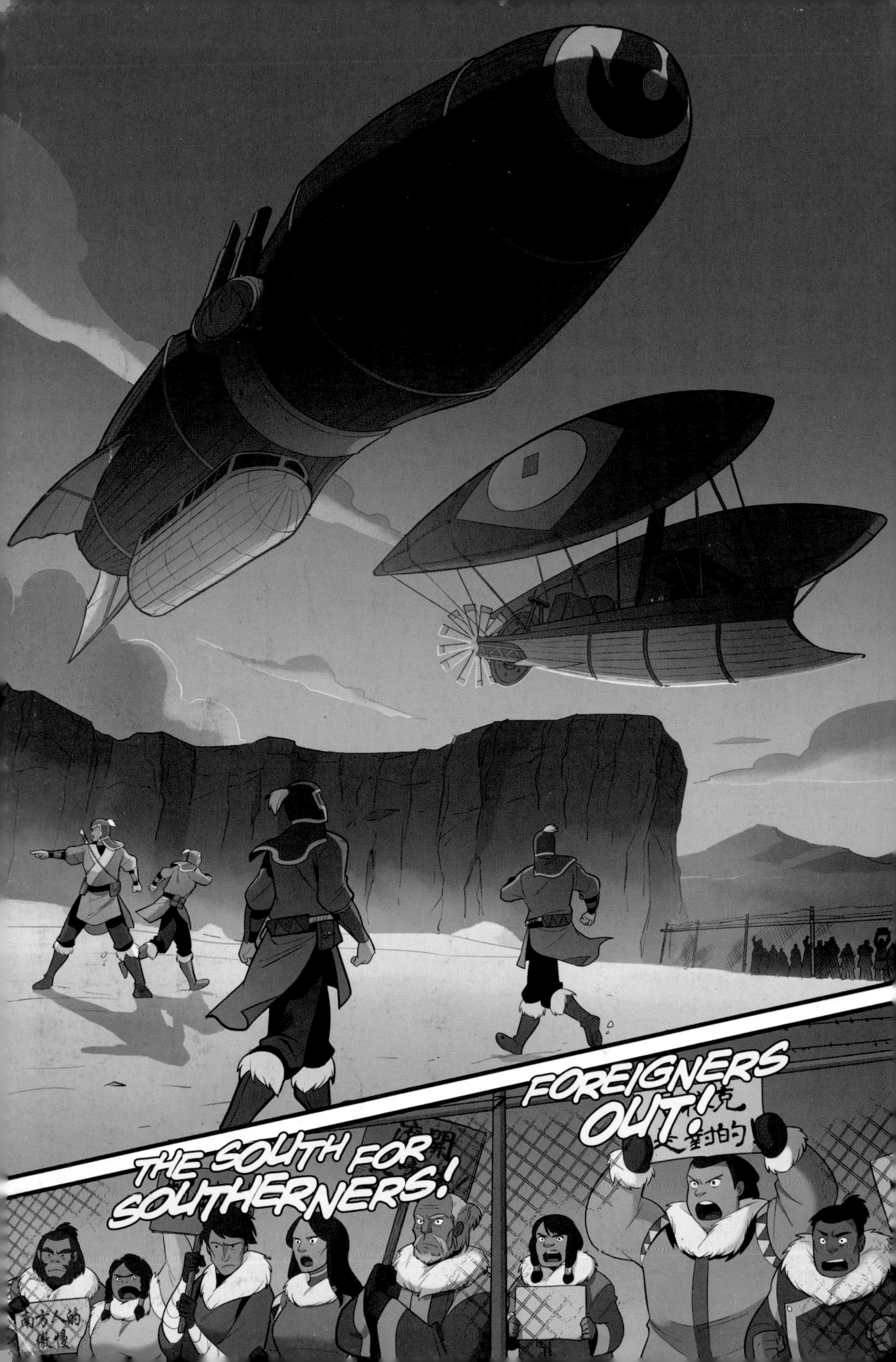
THE SOUTH FOR SOUTHERNERS!
FOREIGNERS OUT!
南方人的
傲慢

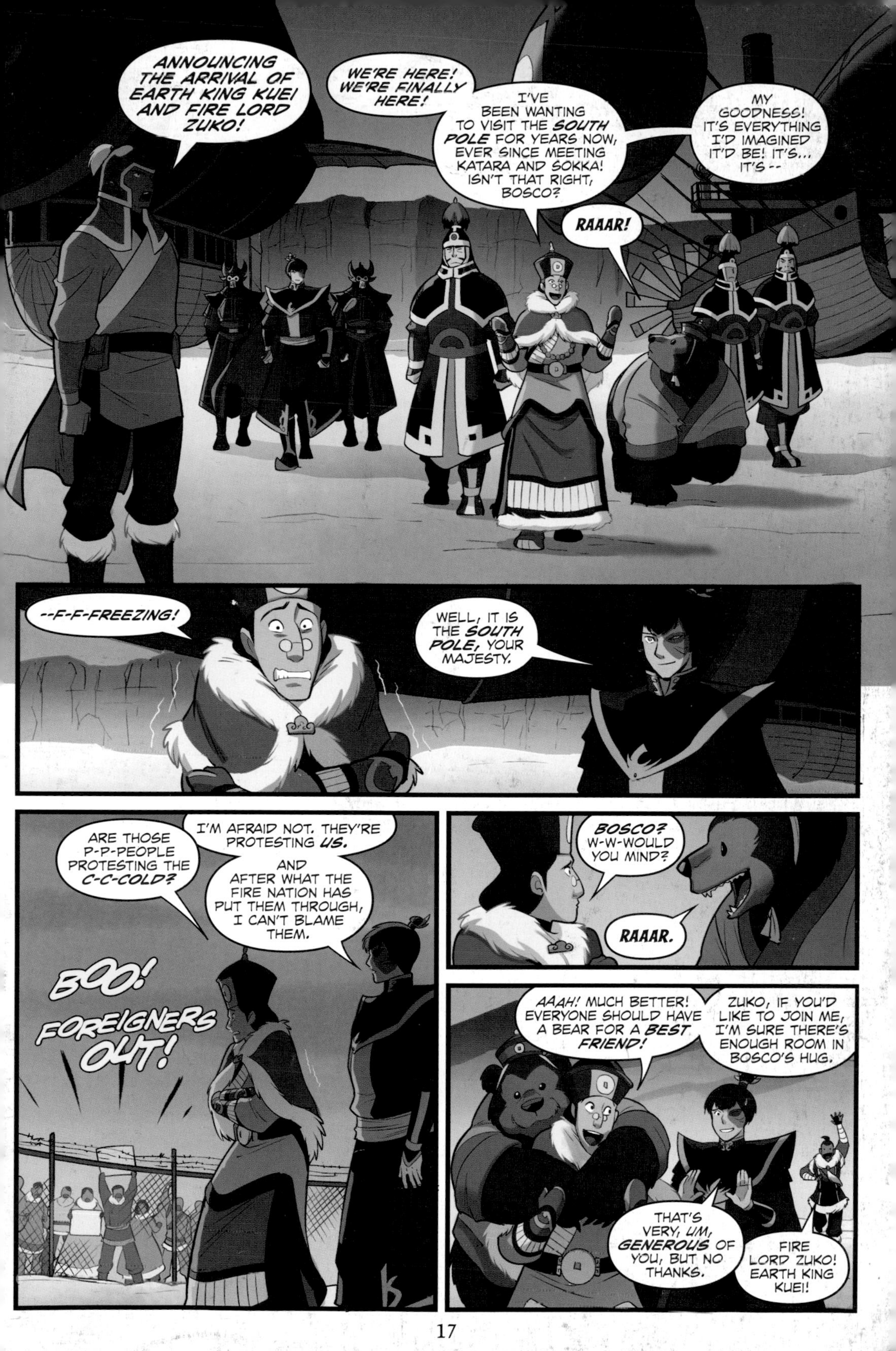
ANNOUNCING THE ARRIVAL OF EARTH KING KUEI AND FIRE LORD ZUKO!
WE'RE HERE! WE'RE FINALLY HERE!
I'VE BEEN WANTING TO VISIT THE SOUTH POLE FOR YEARS NOW, EVER SINCE MEETING KATARA AND SOKKA! ISN'T THAT RIGHT, BOSCO?
MY GOODNESS! IT'S EVERYTHING I'D IMAGINED IT'D BE! IT'S... IT'S --
RAAAR!
--F-F-FREEZING!
WELL, IT IS THE SOUTH POLE, YOUR MAJESTY.
ARE THOSE P-P-PEOPLE PROTESTING THE C-C-COLD?
I'M AFRAID NOT. THEY'RE PROTESTING US.
AND AFTER WHAT THE FIRE NATION HAS PUT THEM THROUGH, I CAN'T BLAME THEM.
BOO!
FOREIGNERS OUT!
BOSCO? W-W-WOULD YOU MIND?
RAAAR.
AAAH! MUCH BETTER! EVERYONE SHOULD HAVE A BEAR FOR A BEST FRIEND!
ZUKO, IF YOU'D LIKE TO JOIN ME, I'M SURE THERE'S ENOUGH ROOM IN BOSCO'S HUG.
THAT'S VERY, UM, GENEROUS OF YOU, BUT NO THANKS.
FIRE LORD ZUKO! EARTH KING KUEI!

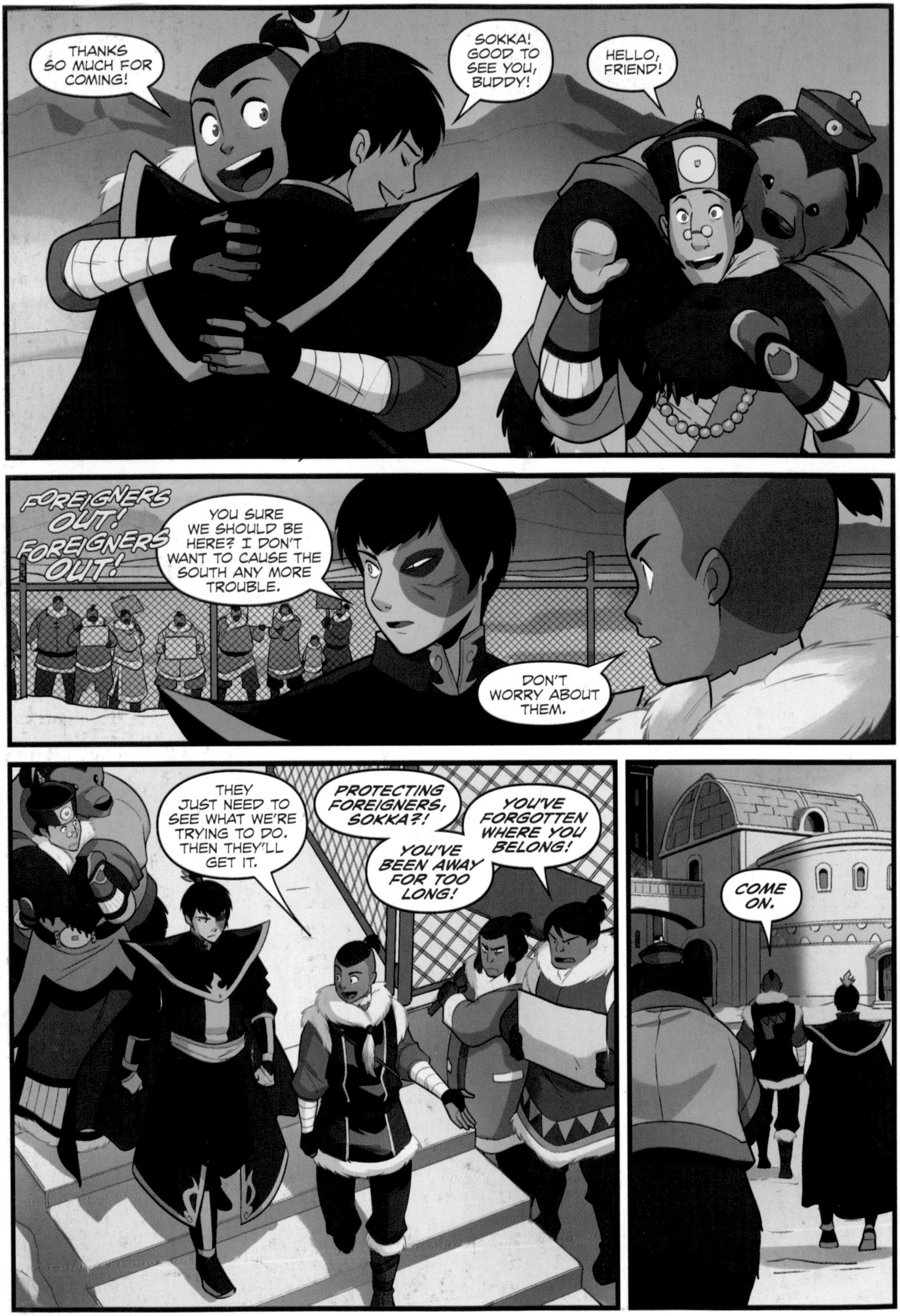

THANKS SO MUCH FOR COMING!
SOKKA! GOOD TO SEE YOU, BUDDY!
HELLO, FRIEND!
FOREIGNERS OUT! FOREIGNERS OUT!
YOU SURE WE SHOULD BE HERE? I DON'T WANT TO CAUSE THE SOUTH ANY MORE TROUBLE.
DON'T WORRY ABOUT THEM.
THEY JUST NEED TO SEE WHAT WE'RE TRYING TO DO. THEN THEY'LL GET IT.
PROTECTING FOREIGNERS, SOKKA?!
YOU'VE BEEN AWAY FOR TOO LONG!
YOU'VE FORGOTTEN WHERE YOU BELONG!
COME ON.

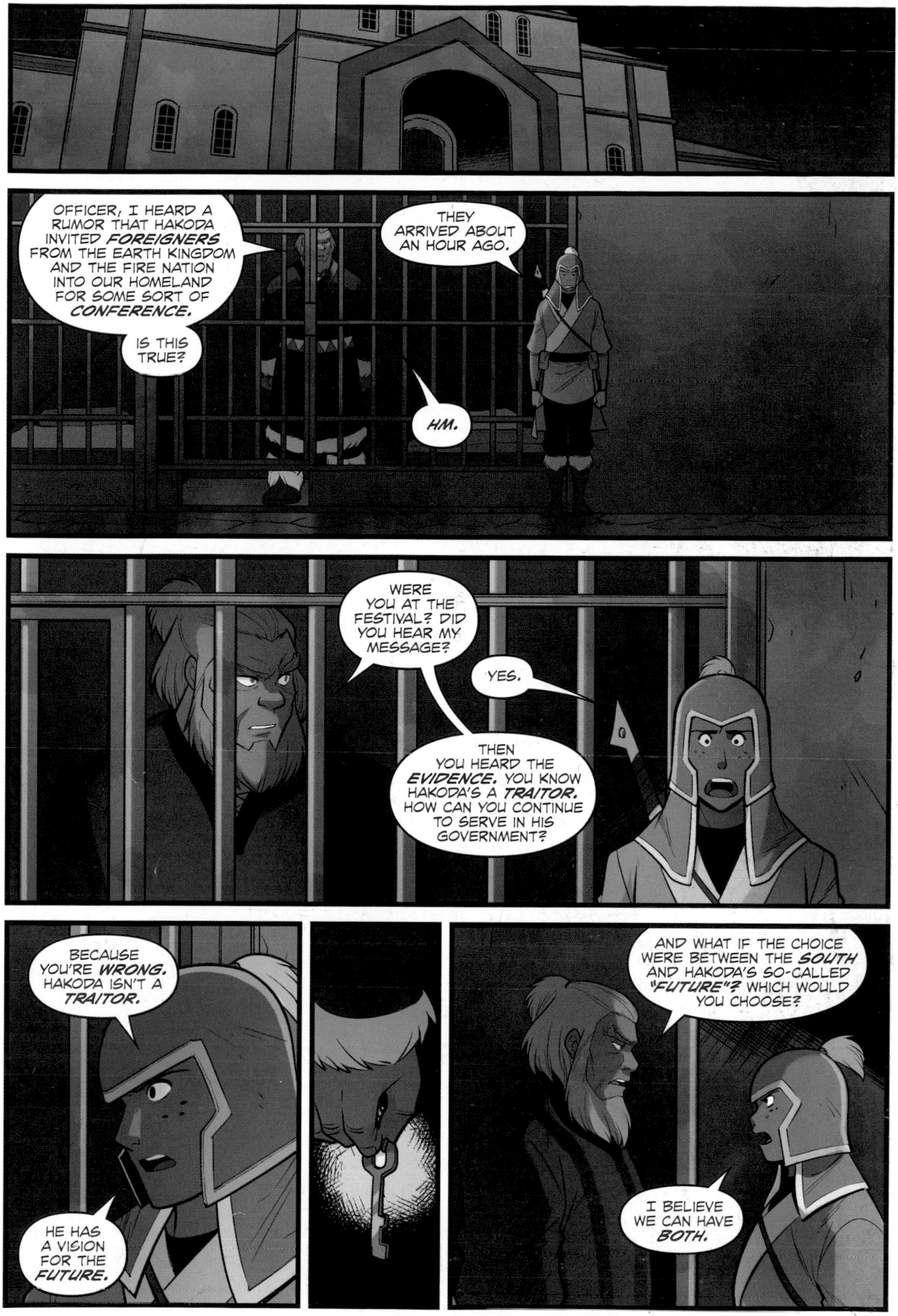
OFFICER, I HEARD A RUMOR THAT HAKODA INVITED FOREIGNERS FROM THE EARTH KINGDOM AND THE FIRE NATION INTO OUR HOMELAND FOR SOME SORT OF CONFERENCE.
IS THIS TRUE?
THEY ARRIVED ABOUT AN HOUR AGO.
HM.
WERE YOU AT THE FESTIVAL? DID YOU HEAR MY MESSAGE?
YES.
THEN YOU HEARD THE EVIDENCE. YOU KNOW HAKODA'S A TRAITOR. HOW CAN YOU CONTINUE TO SERVE IN HIS GOVERNMENT?
BECAUSE YOU'RE WRONG. HAKODA ISN'T A TRAITOR.
HE HAS A VISION FOR THE FUTURE.
AND WHAT IF THE CHOICE WERE BETWEEN THE SOUTH AND HAKODA'S SO-CALLED "FUTURE"? WHICH WOULD YOU CHOOSE?
I BELIEVE WE CAN HAVE BOTH.

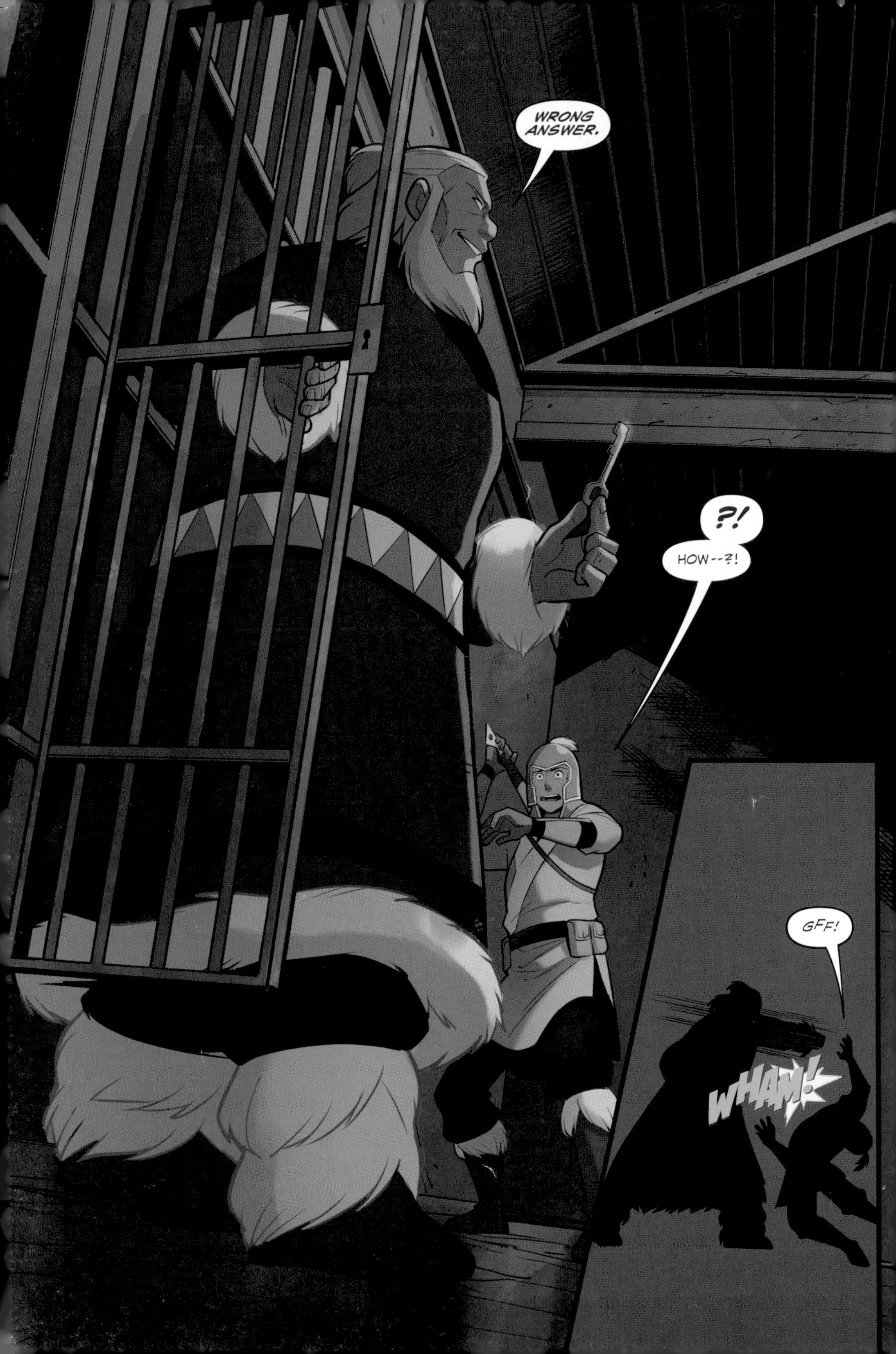
WRONG ANSWER.
?!
HOW--?!
GFF!
WHAM!

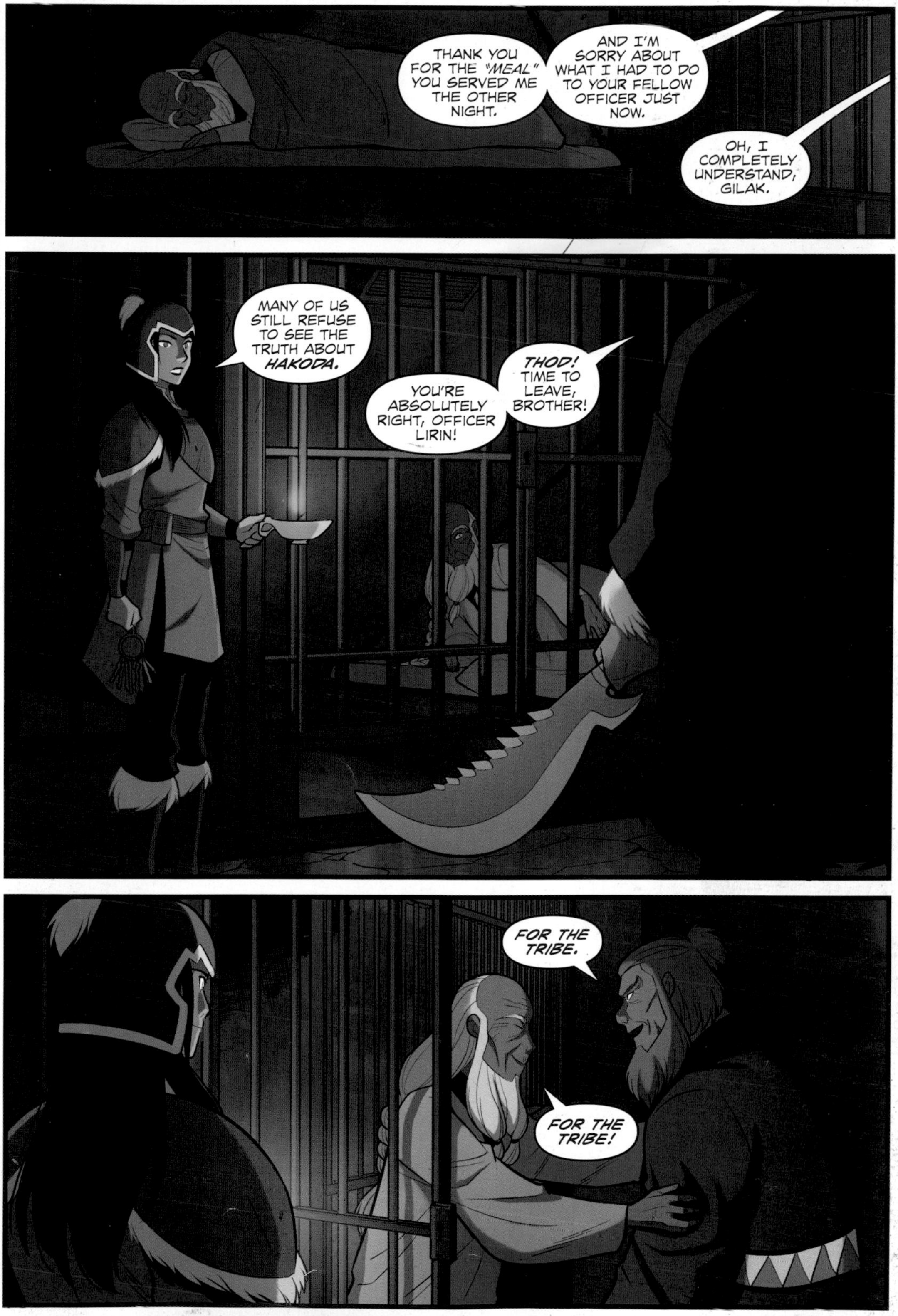
THANK YOU FOR THE "MEAL" YOU SERVED ME THE OTHER NIGHT.
AND I'M SORRY ABOUT WHAT I HAD TO DO TO YOUR FELLOW OFFICER JUST NOW.
OH, I COMPLETELY UNDERSTAND, GILAK.
MANY OF US STILL REFUSE TO SEE THE TRUTH ABOUT HAKODA.
YOU'RE ABSOLUTELY RIGHT, OFFICER LIRIN!
THOD! TIME TO LEAVE, BROTHER!
FOR THE TRIBE.
FOR THE TRIBE!

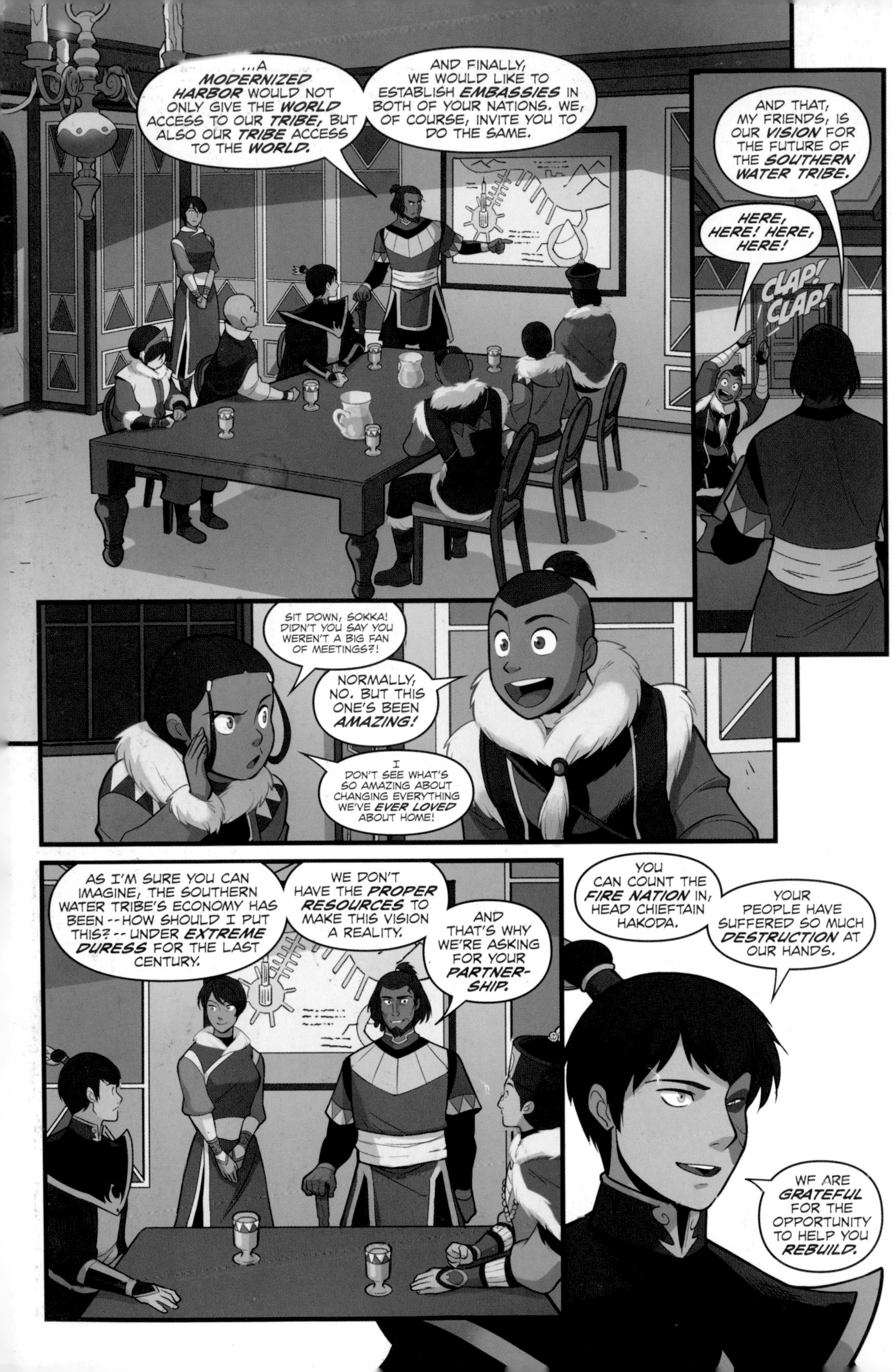

...A MODERNIZED HARBOR WOULD NOT ONLY GIVE THE WORLD ACCESS TO OUR TRIBE, BUT ALSO OUR TRIBE ACCESS TO THE WORLD.
AND FINALLY, WE WOULD LIKE TO ESTABLISH EMBASSIES IN BOTH OF YOUR NATIONS. WE, OF COURSE, INVITE YOU TO DO THE SAME.
AND THAT, MY FRIENDS, IS OUR VISION FOR THE FUTURE OF THE SOUTHERN WATER TRIBE.
HERE, HERE! HERE, HERE!
CLAP! CLAP!
SIT DOWN, SOKKA! DIDN'T YOU SAY YOU WEREN'T A BIG FAN OF MEETINGS?!
NORMALLY, NO. BUT THIS ONE'S BEEN AMAZING!
I DON'T SEE WHAT'S SO AMAZING ABOUT CHANGING EVERYTHING WE'VE EVER LOVED ABOUT HOME!
AS I'M SURE YOU CAN IMAGINE, THE SOUTHERN WATER TRIBE'S ECONOMY HAS BEEN--HOW SHOULD I PUT THIS?--UNDER EXTREME DURESS FOR THE LAST CENTURY.
WE DON'T HAVE THE PROPER RESOURCES TO MAKE THIS VISION A REALITY.
AND THAT'S WHY WE'RE ASKING FOR YOUR PARTNERSHIP.
YOU CAN COUNT THE FIRE NATION IN, HEAD CHIEFTAIN HAKODA.
YOUR PEOPLE HAVE SUFFERED SO MUCH DESTRUCTION AT OUR HANDS.
WE ARE GRATEFUL FOR THE OPPORTUNITY TO HELP YOU REBUILD.

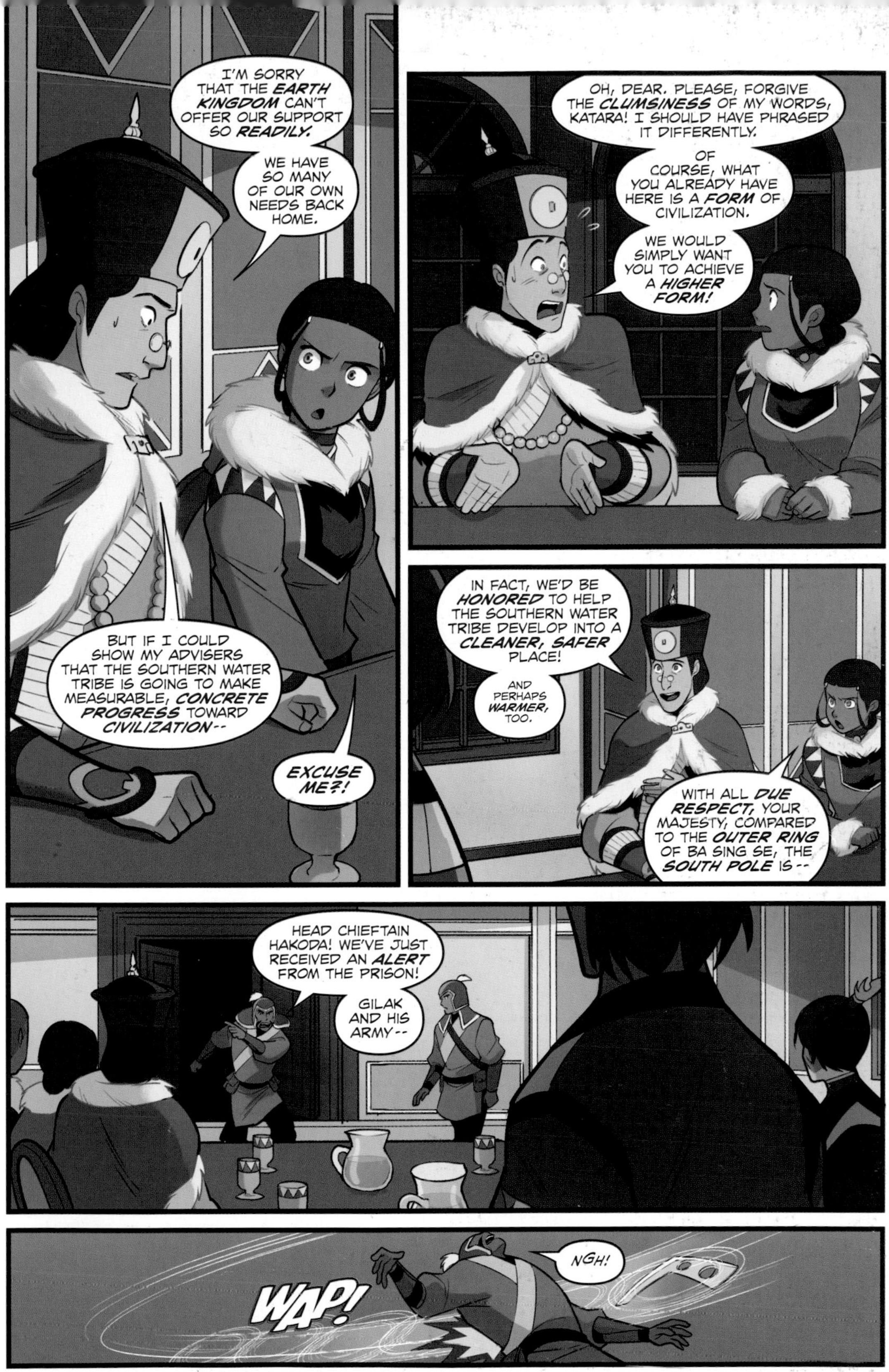
I'M SORRY THAT THE EARTH KINGDOM CAN'T OFFER OUR SUPPORT SO READILY.
WE HAVE SO MANY OF OUR OWN NEEDS BACK HOME.
BUT IF I COULD SHOW MY ADVISERS THAT THE SOUTHERN WATER TRIBE IS GOING TO MAKE MEASURABLE, CONCRETE PROGRESS TOWARD CIVILIZATION--
EXCUSE ME?!
OH, DEAR. PLEASE, FORGIVE THE CLUMSINESS OF MY WORDS, KATARA! I SHOULD HAVE PHRASED IT DIFFERENTLY.
OF COURSE, WHAT YOU ALREADY HAVE HERE IS A FORM OF CIVILIZATION.
WE WOULD SIMPLY WANT YOU TO ACHIEVE A HIGHER FORM!
IN FACT, WE'D BE HONORED TO HELP THE SOUTHERN WATER TRIBE DEVELOP INTO A CLEANER, SAFER PLACE!
AND PERHAPS WARMER, TOO.
WITH ALL DUE RESPECT, YOUR MAJESTY, COMPARED TO THE OUTER RING OF BA SING SE, THE SOUTH POLE IS--
HEAD CHIEFTAIN HAKODA! WE'VE JUST RECEIVED AN ALERT FROM THE PRISON!
GILAK AND HIS ARMY--
WAP!
NGH!

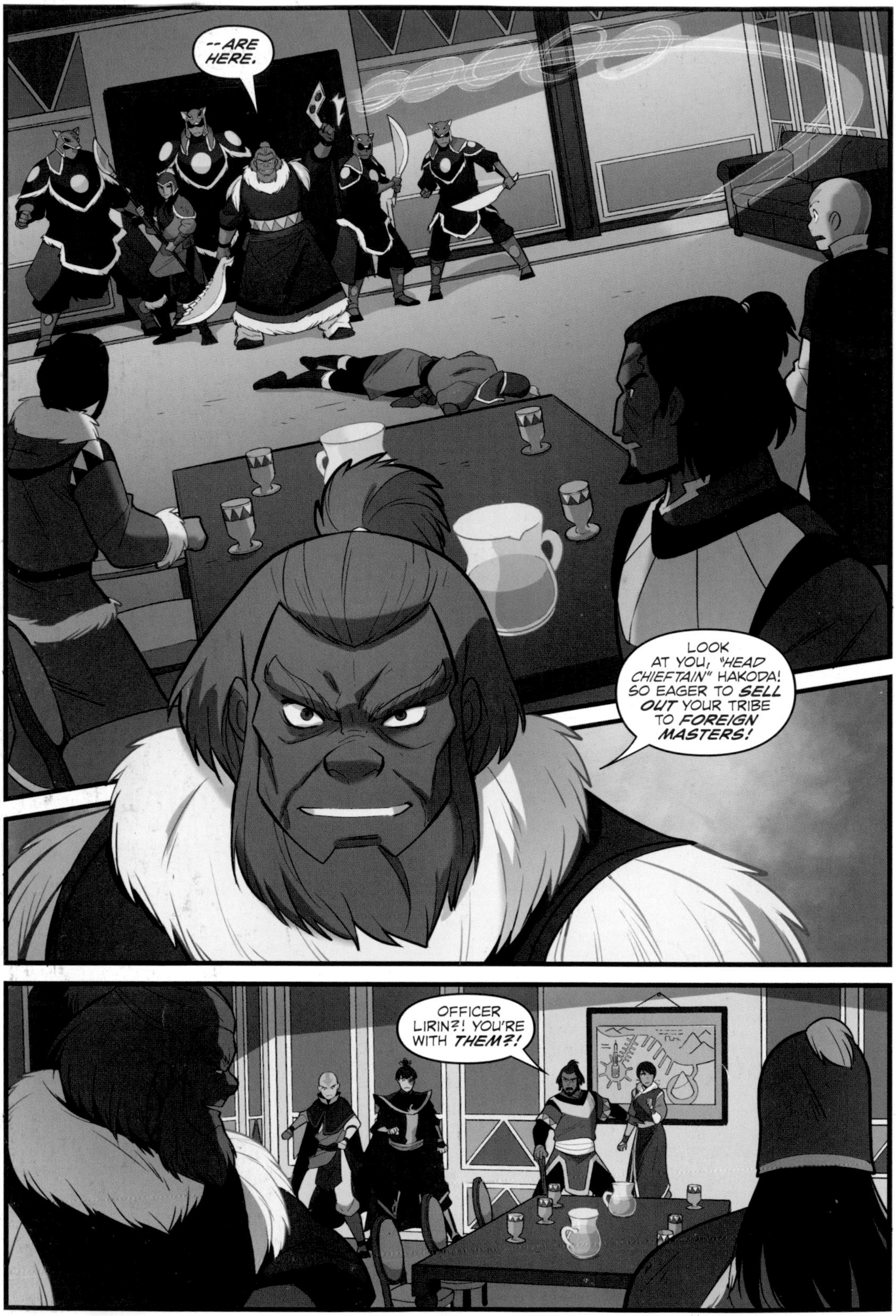
--ARE HERE.
LOOK AT YOU, "HEAD CHIEFTAIN" HAKODA! SO EAGER TO SELL OUT YOUR TRIBE TO FOREIGN MASTERS!
OFFICER LIRIN?! YOU'RE WITH THEM?!

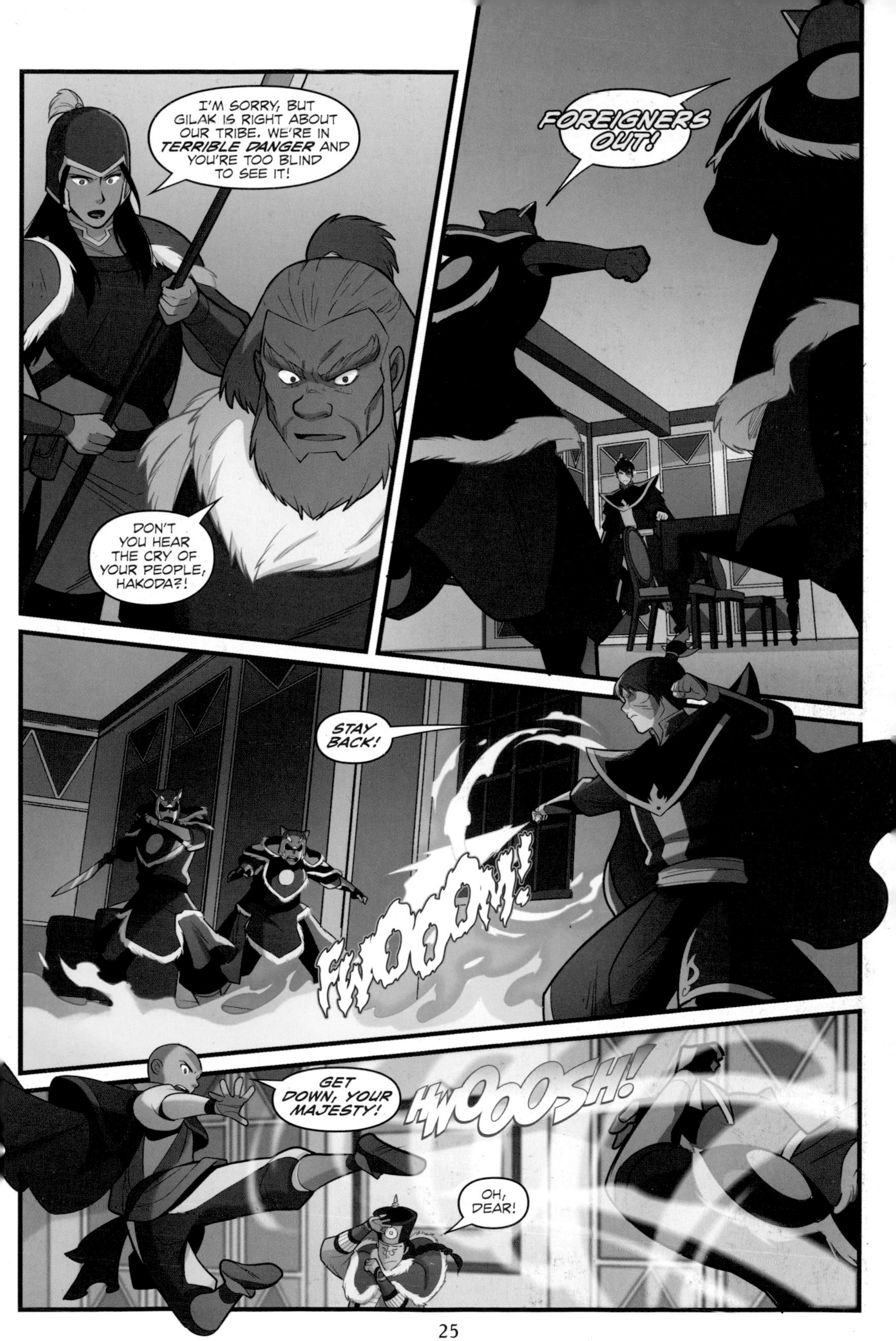
I'M SORRY, BUT GILAK IS RIGHT ABOUT OUR TRIBE. WE'RE IN TERRIBLE DANGER AND YOU'RE TOO BLIND TO SEE IT!
DON'T YOU HEAR THE CRY OF YOUR PEOPLE, HAKODA?!
FOREIGNERS OUT!
STAY BACK!
FWOOOM!
GET DOWN, YOUR MAJESTY!
HWOOOSH!
OH, DEAR!

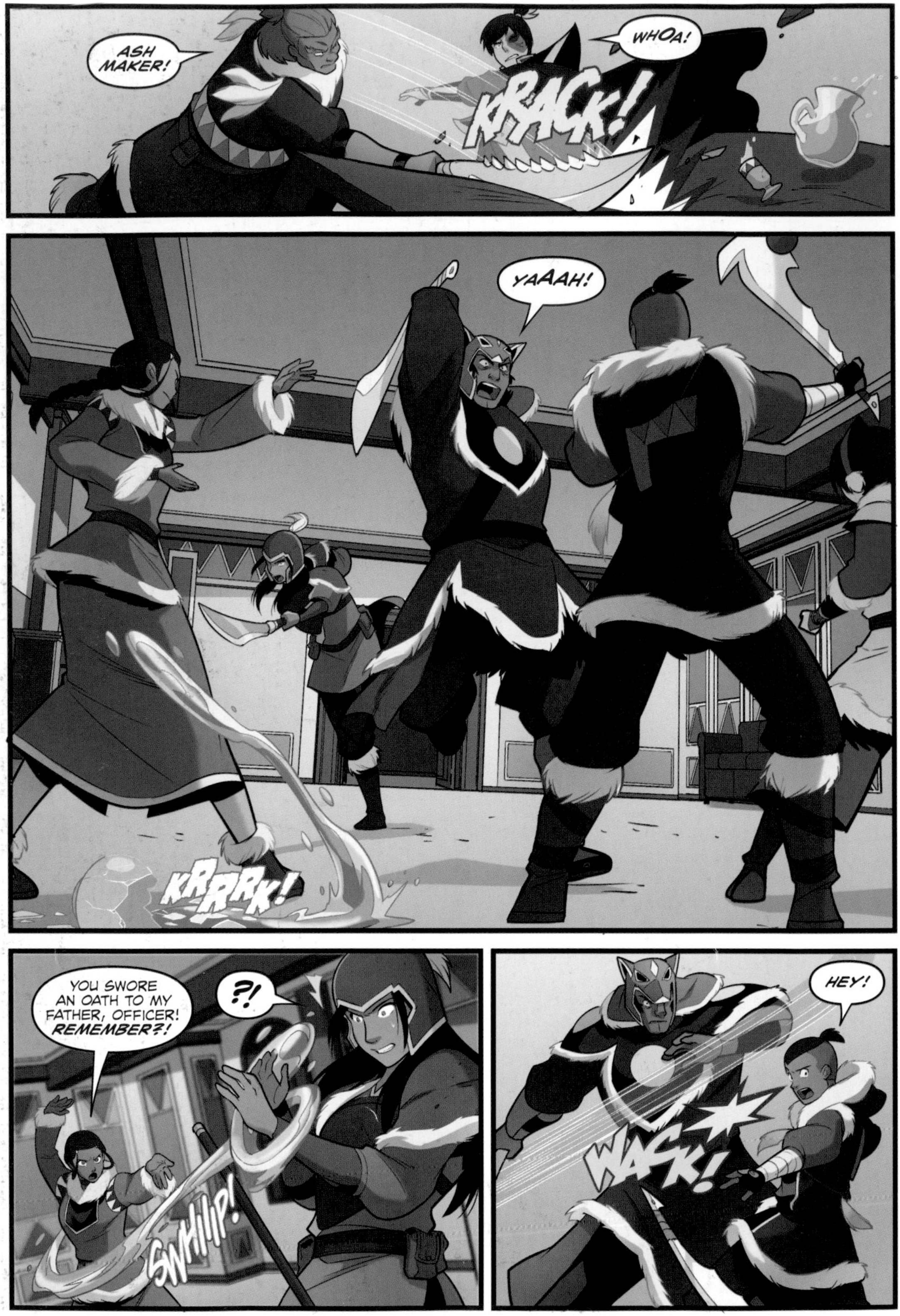
ASH MAKER!
WHOA!
KRACK!
YAAAH!
KRRRK!
YOU SWORE AN OATH TO MY FATHER, OFFICER! REMEMBER?!
?!
SWHIIP!
HEY!
WACK!

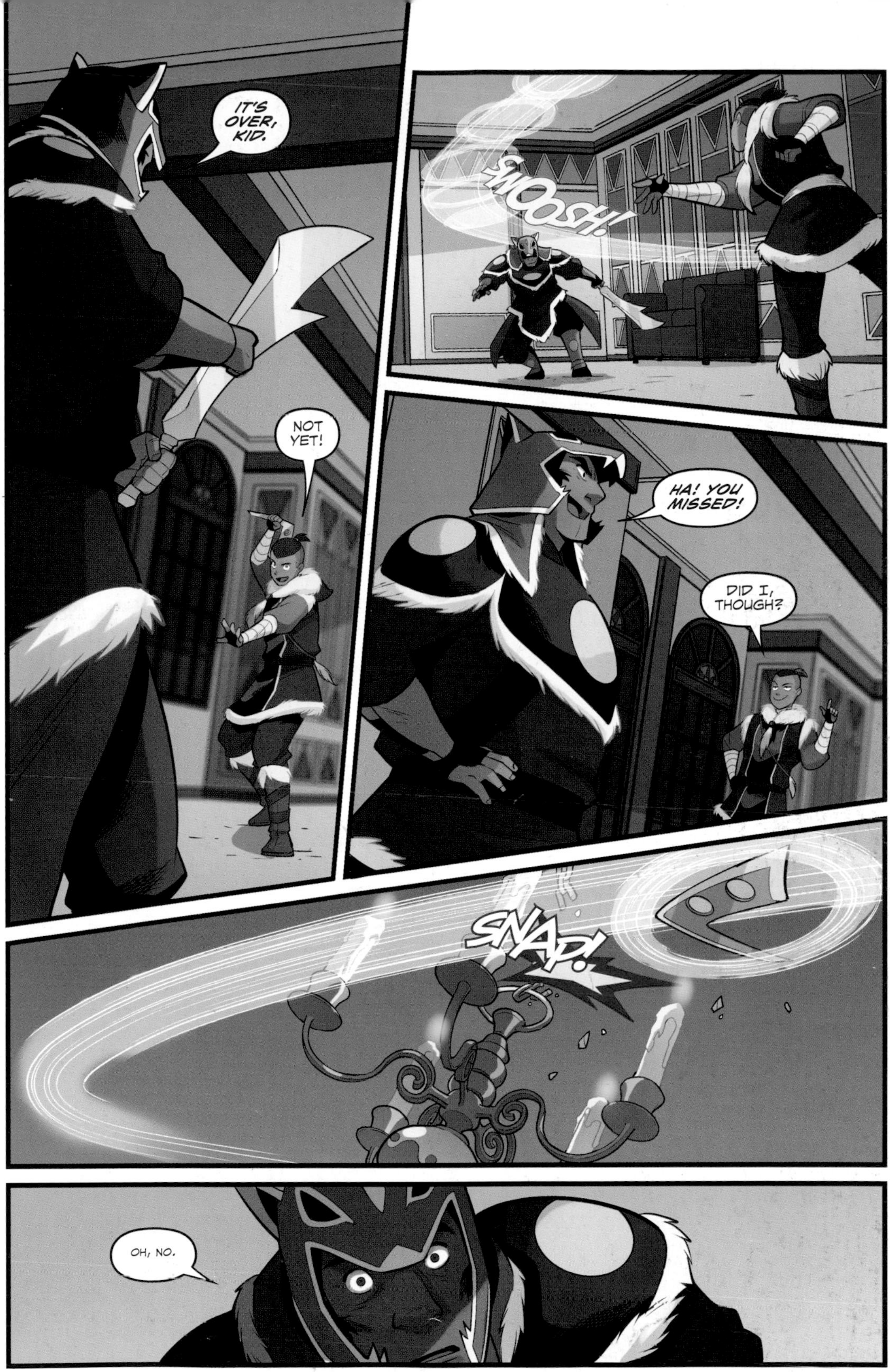
IT'S OVER, KID.
SWOOSH!
NOT YET!
HA! YOU MISSED!
DID I, THOUGH?
SNAP!
OH, NO.

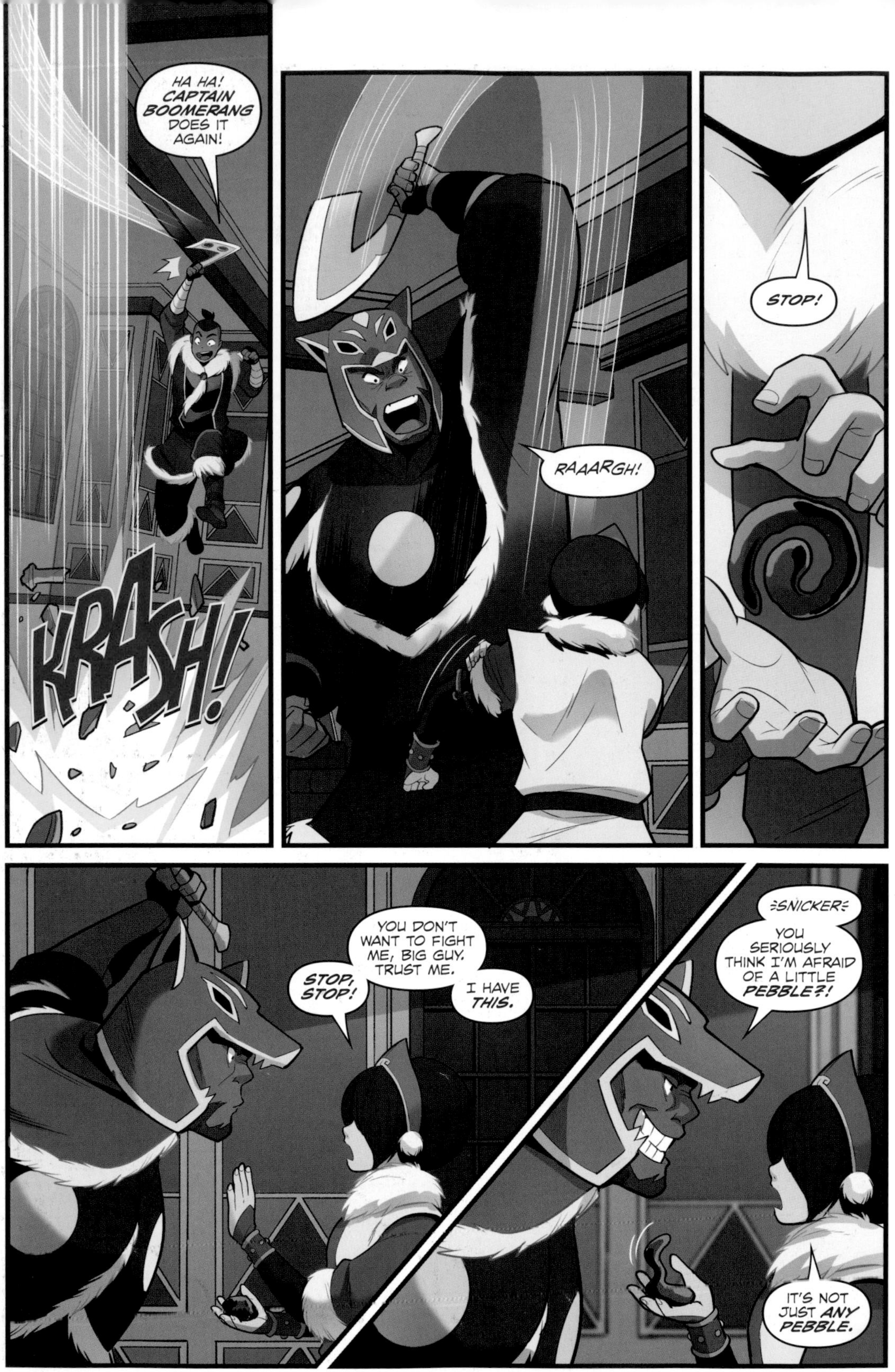
HA HA! CAPTAIN BOOMERANG DOES IT AGAIN!
KRASH!
RAAARGH!
STOP!
STOP, STOP!
YOU DON'T WANT TO FIGHT ME, BIG GUY. TRUST ME.
I HAVE THIS.
=SNICKER=
YOU SERIOUSLY THINK I'M AFRAID OF A LITTLE PEBBLE?!
IT'S NOT JUST ANY PEBBLE.

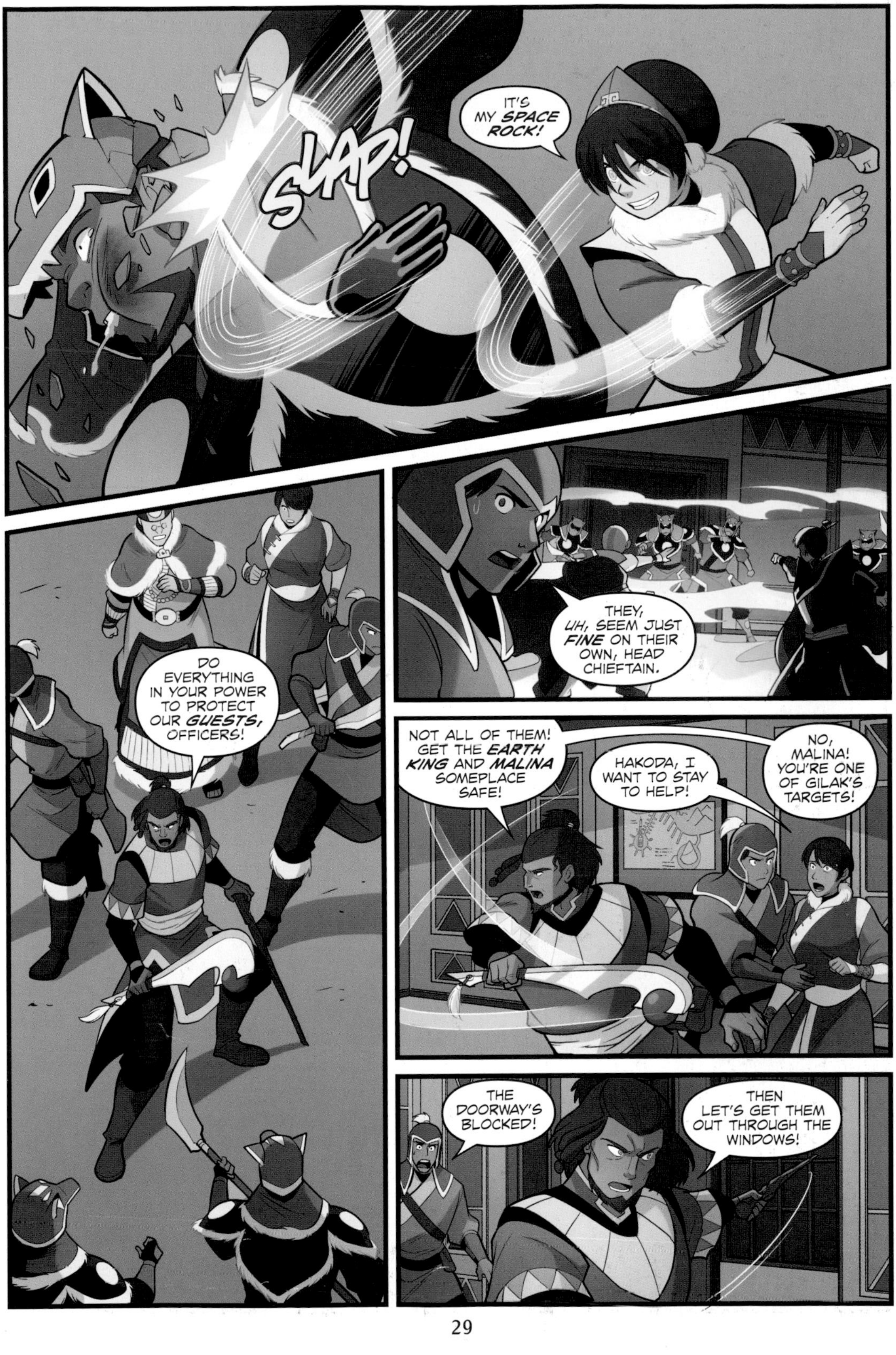
SLAP!
IT'S MY SPACE ROCK!
THEY, UH, SEEM JUST FINE ON THEIR OWN, HEAD CHIEFTAIN.
DO EVERYTHING IN YOUR POWER TO PROTECT OUR GUESTS, OFFICERS!
NOT ALL OF THEM! GET THE EARTH KING AND MALINA SOMEPLACE SAFE!
HAKODA, I WANT TO STAY TO HELP!
NO, MALINA! YOU'RE ONE OF GILAK'S TARGETS!
THE DOORWAY'S BLOCKED!
THEN LET'S GET THEM OUT THROUGH THE WINDOWS!

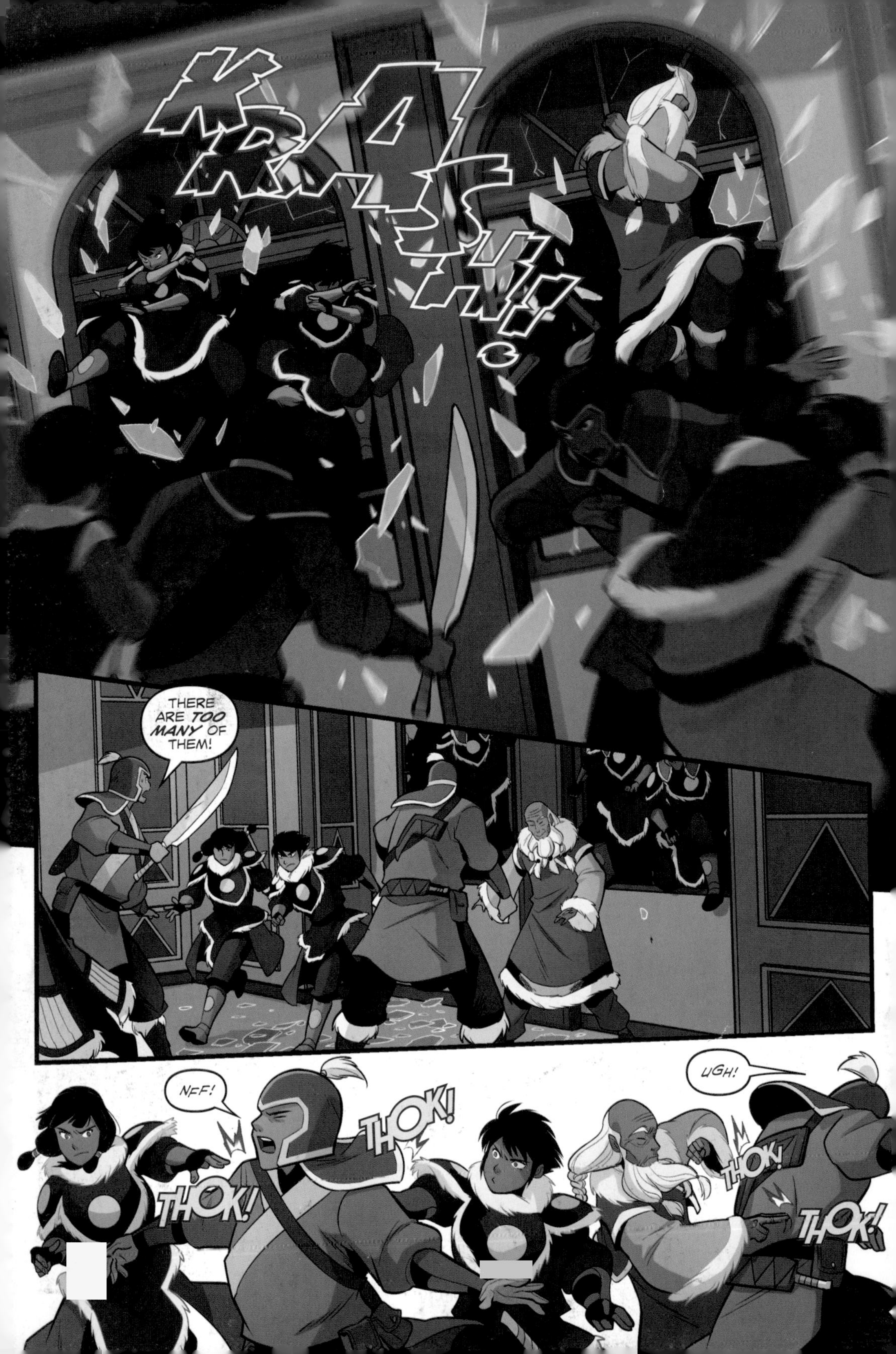

KRASH!!
THERE ARE TOO MANY OF THEM!
NFF!
THOK!
THOK!
UGH!
THOK!
THOK!

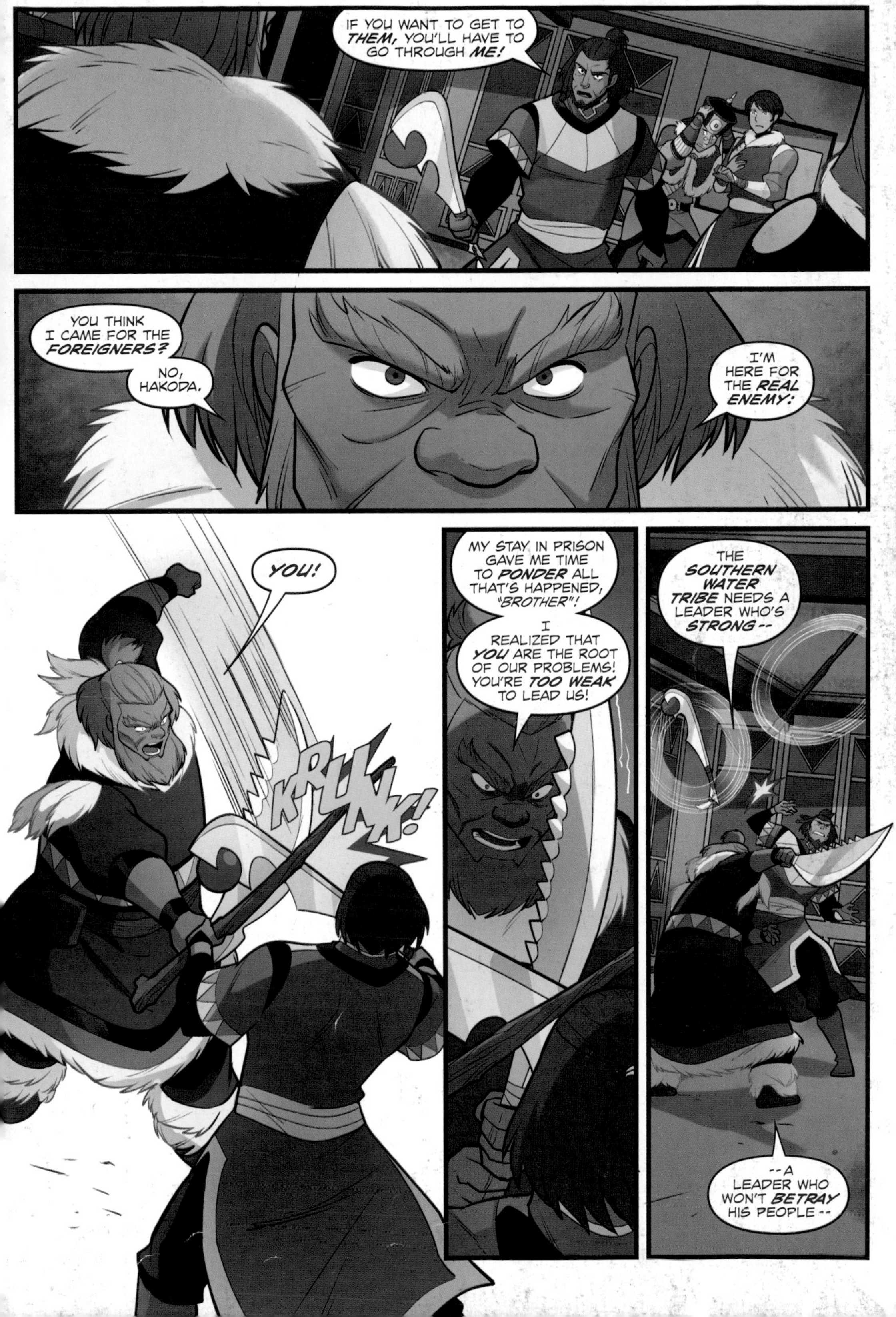
IF YOU WANT TO GET TO THEM, YOU'LL HAVE TO GO THROUGH ME!
YOU THINK I CAME FOR THE FOREIGNERS?
NO, HAKODA.
I'M HERE FOR THE REAL ENEMY:
YOU!
KRUNK!
MY STAY IN PRISON GAVE ME TIME TO PONDER ALL THAT'S HAPPENED, "BROTHER"!
I REALIZED THAT YOU ARE THE ROOT OF OUR PROBLEMS! YOU'RE TOO WEAK TO LEAD US!
THE SOUTHERN WATER TRIBE NEEDS A LEADER WHO'S STRONG --
-- A LEADER WHO WON'T BETRAY HIS PEOPLE --

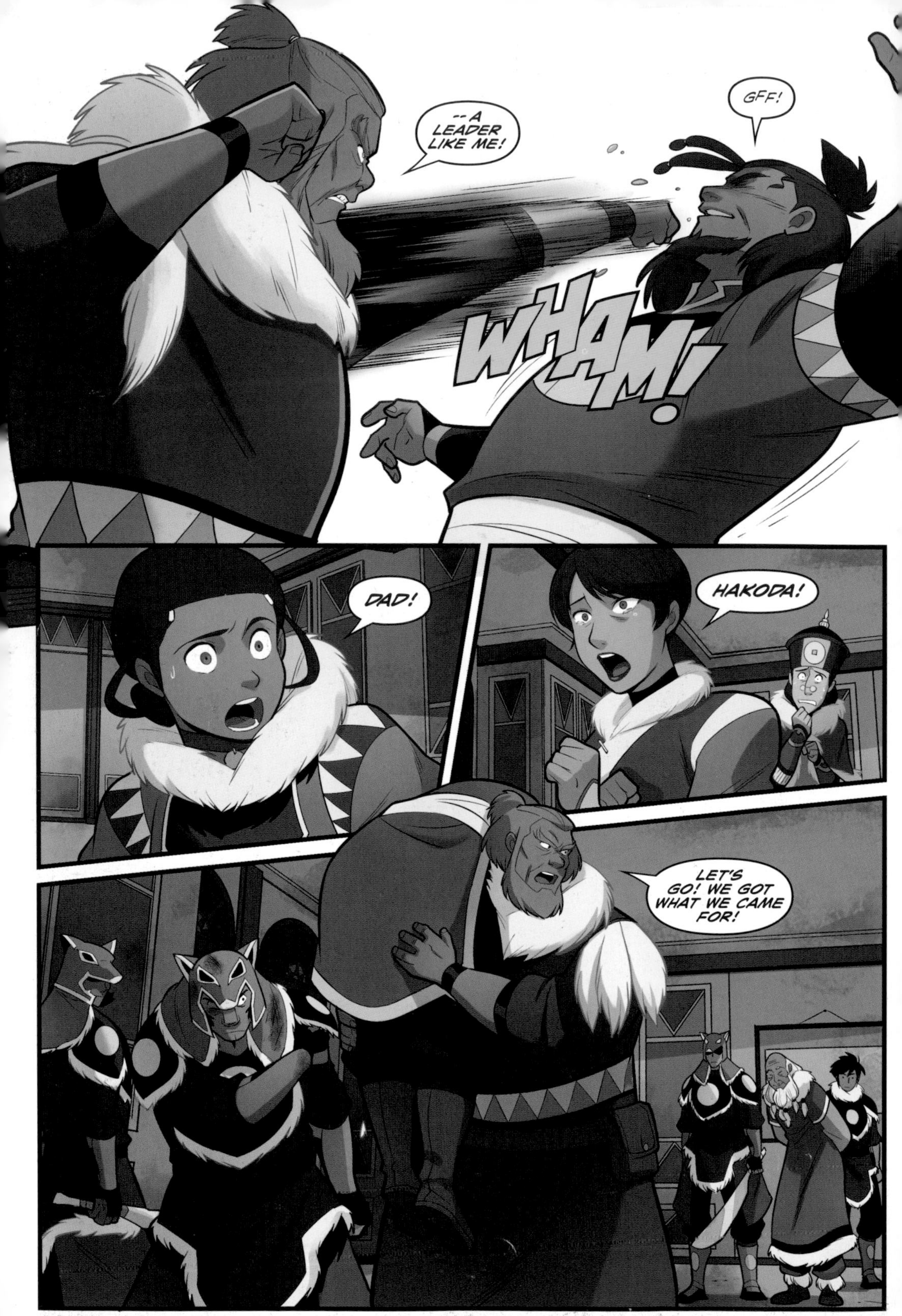
-- A LEADER LIKE ME!
GFF!
WHAM!
DAD!
HAKODA!
LET'S GO! WE GOT WHAT WE CAME FOR!

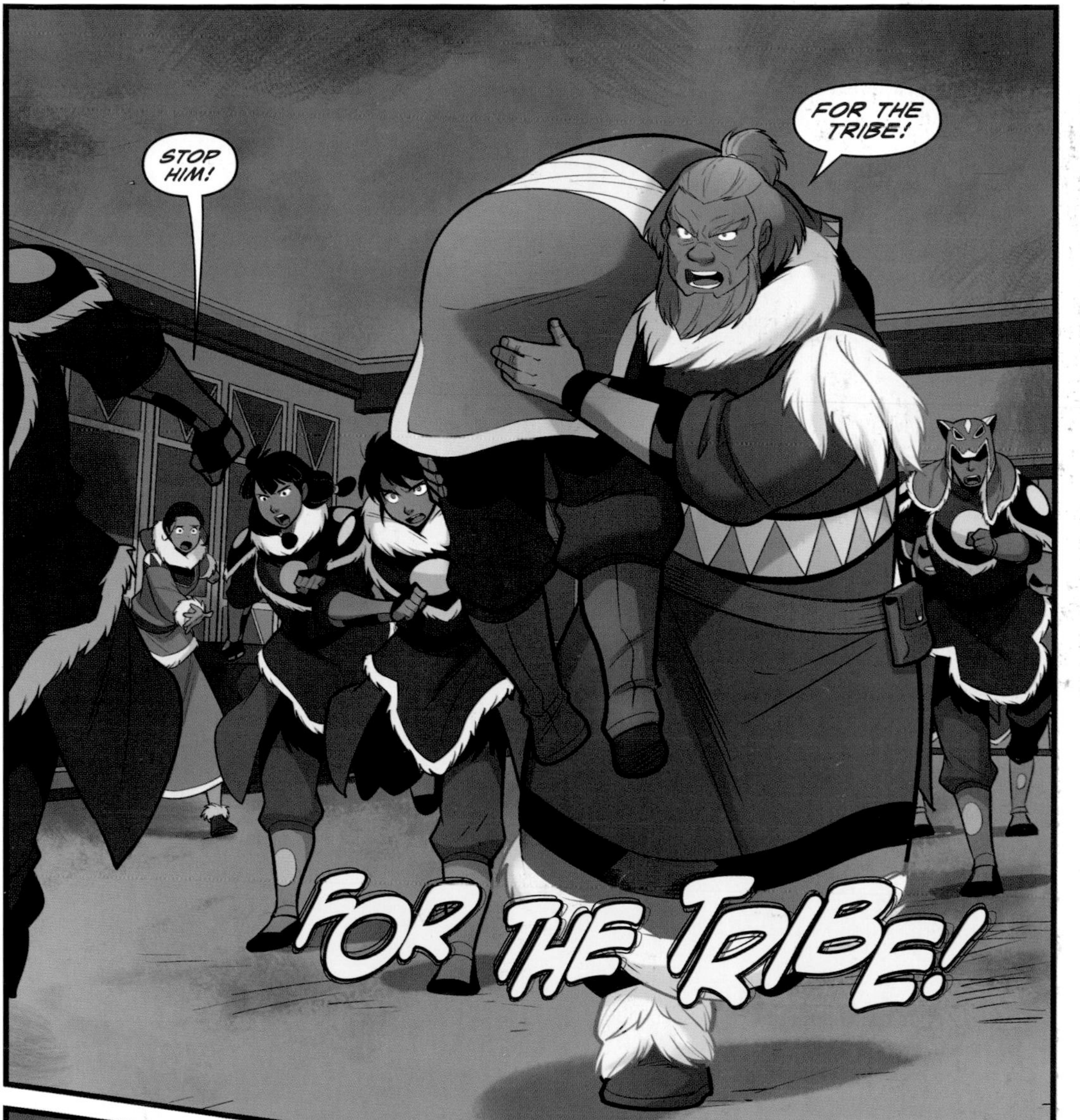
STOP HIM!
FOR THE TRIBE!
FOR THE TRIBE!
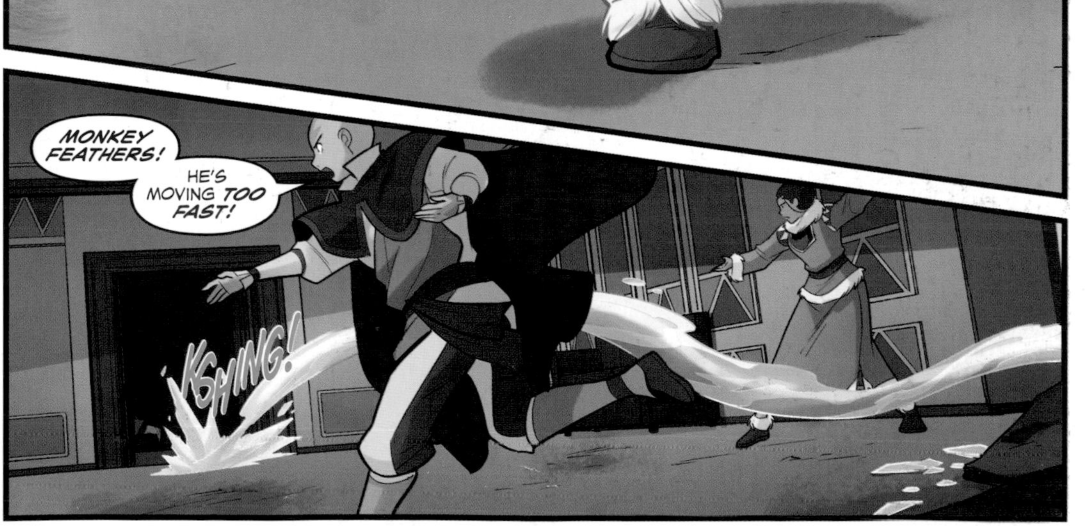
MONKEY FEATHERS!
HE'S MOVING TOO FAST!
KSHING!

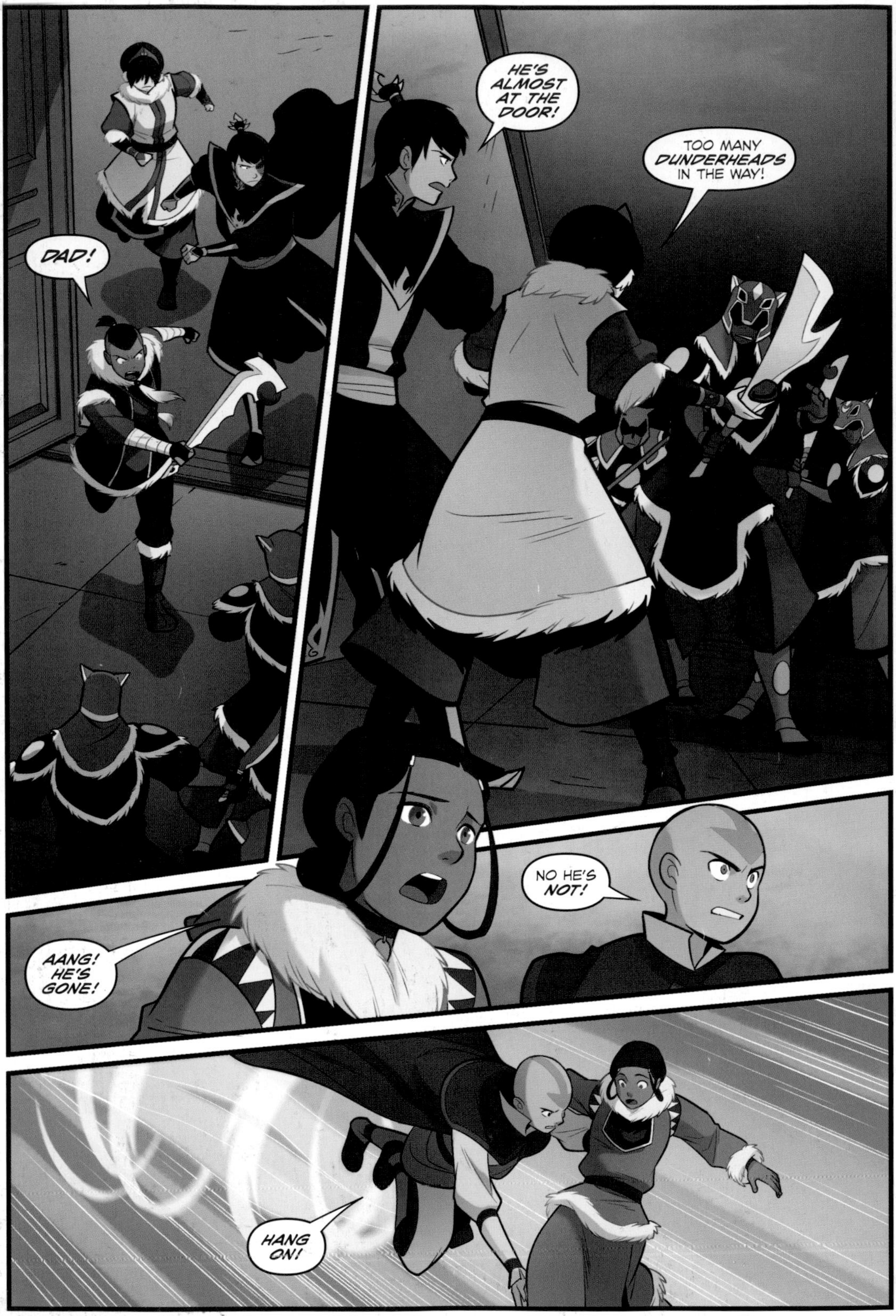

DAD!
HE'S ALMOST AT THE DOOR!
TOO MANY DUNDERHEADS IN THE WAY!
AANG! HE'S GONE!
NO HE'S NOT!
HANG ON!

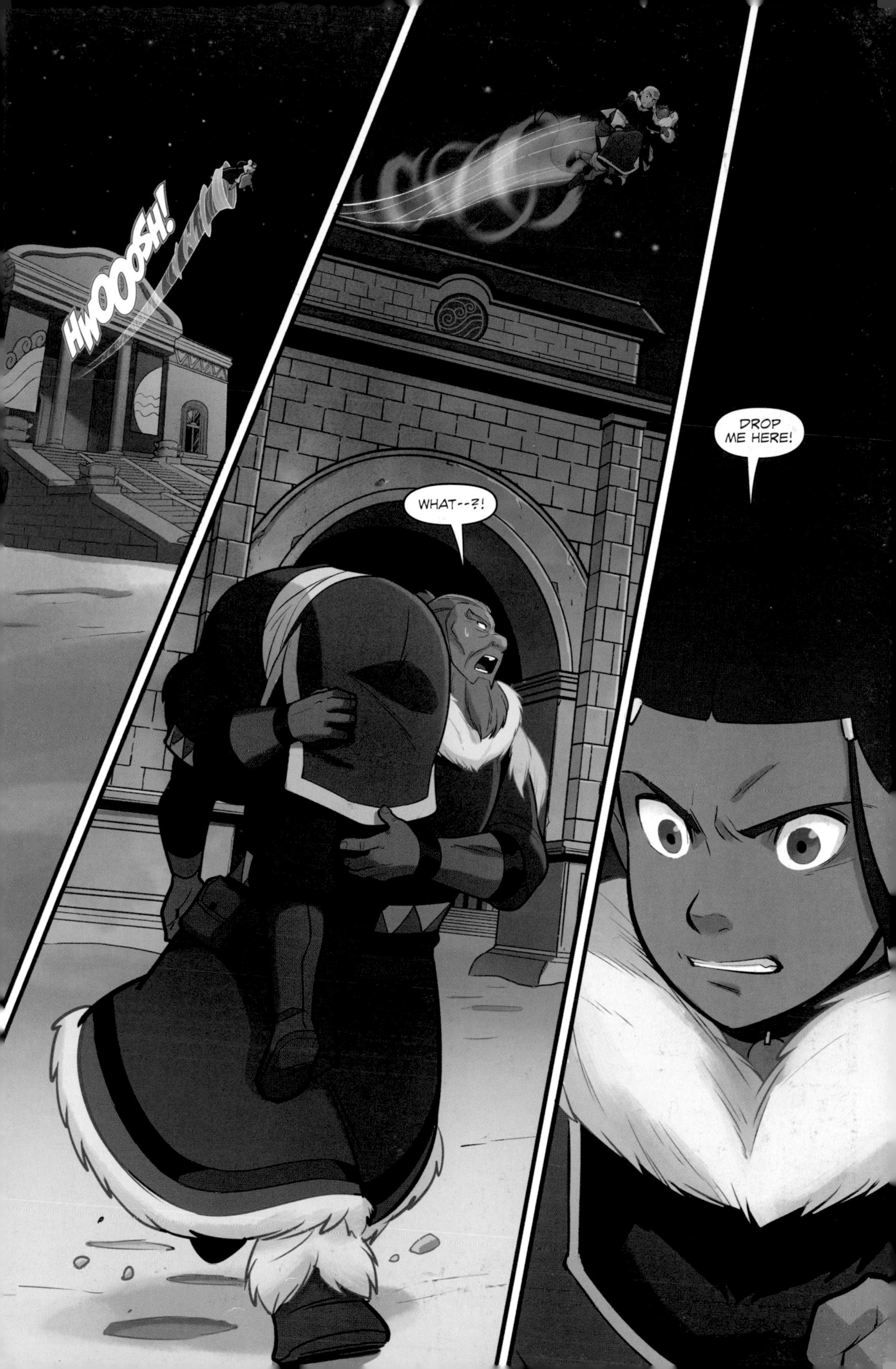
HWOOOSH!
WHAT--?!
DROP ME HERE!

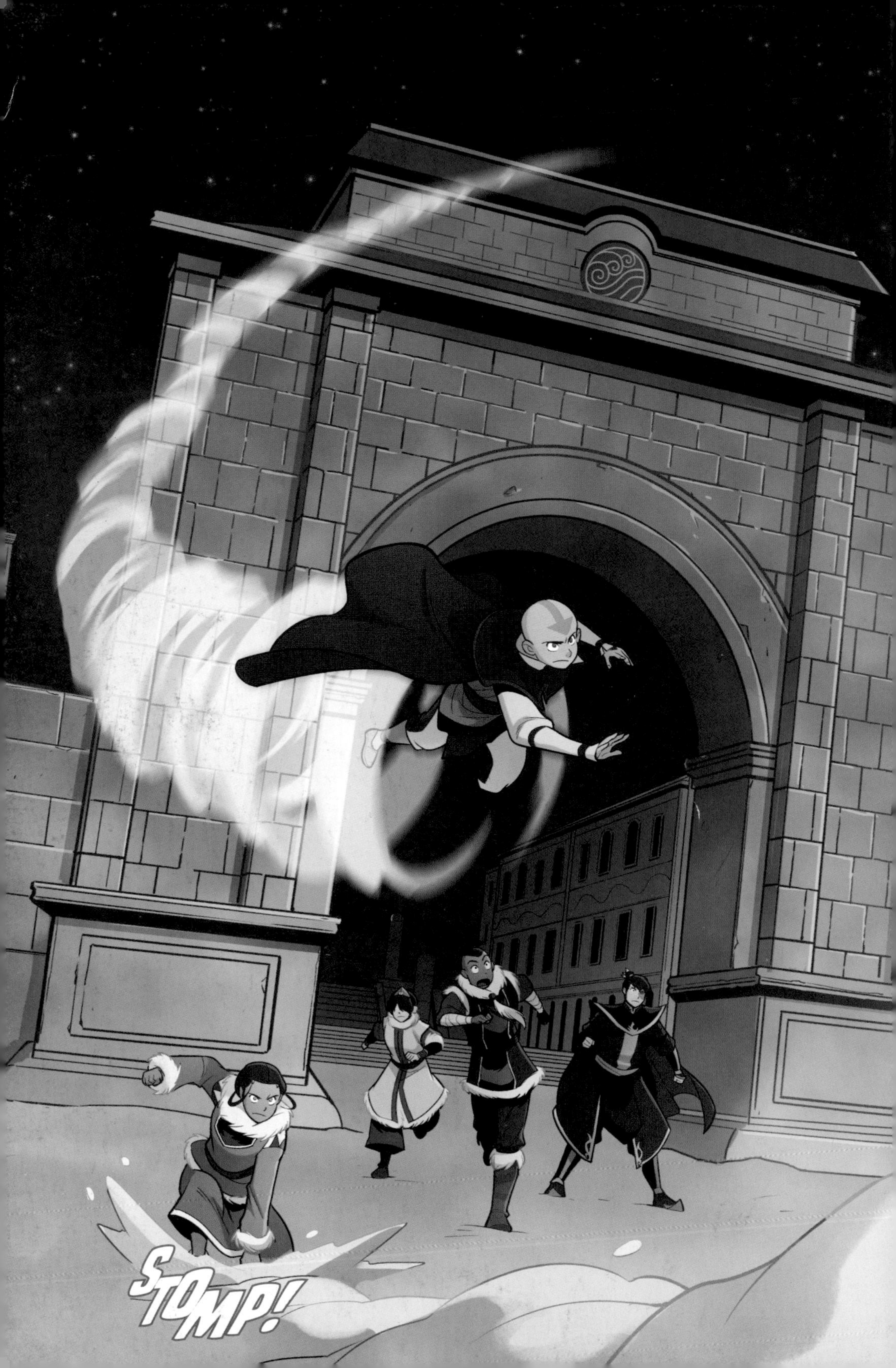
STOMP!

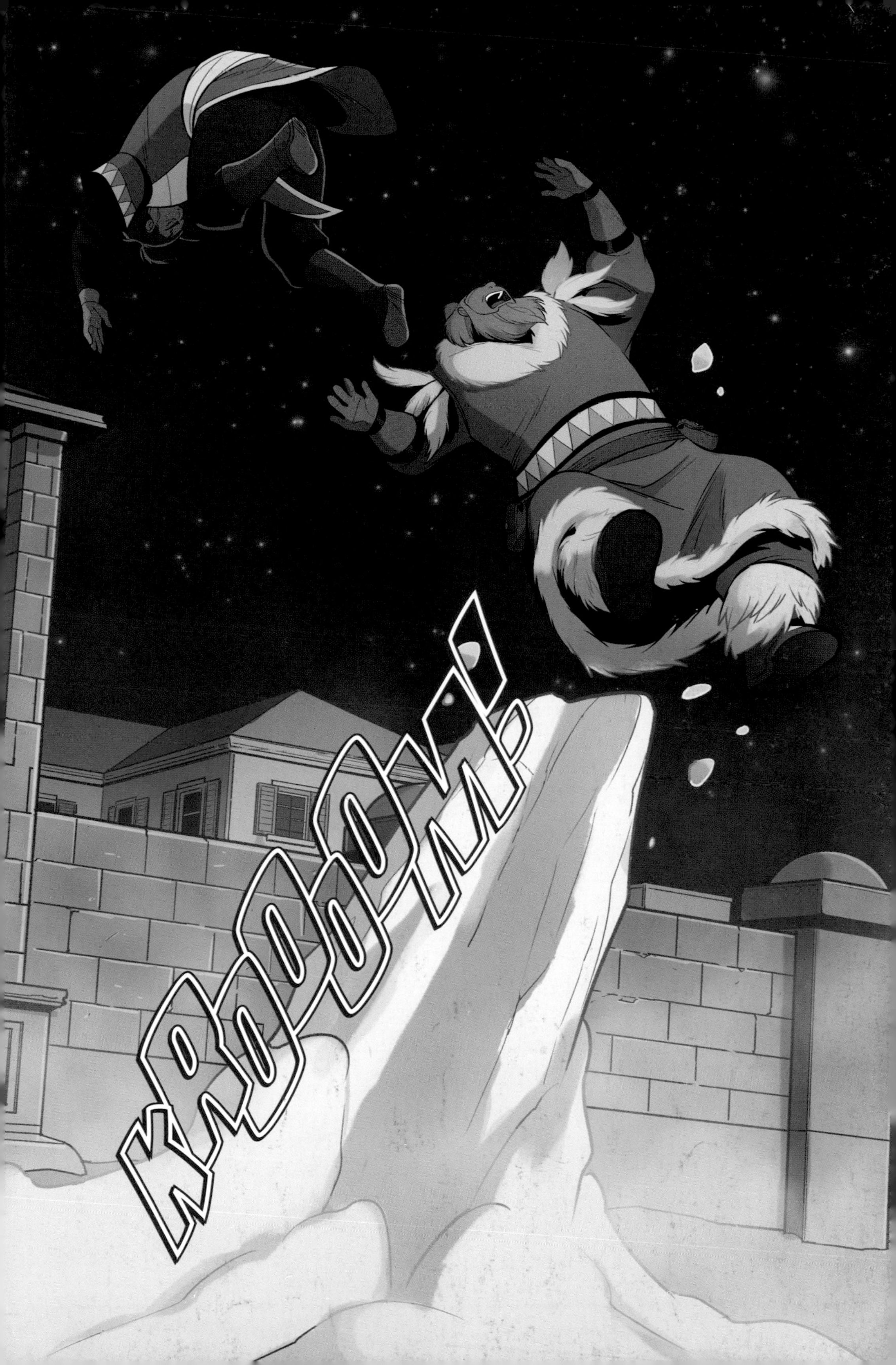
KROOOOSH!

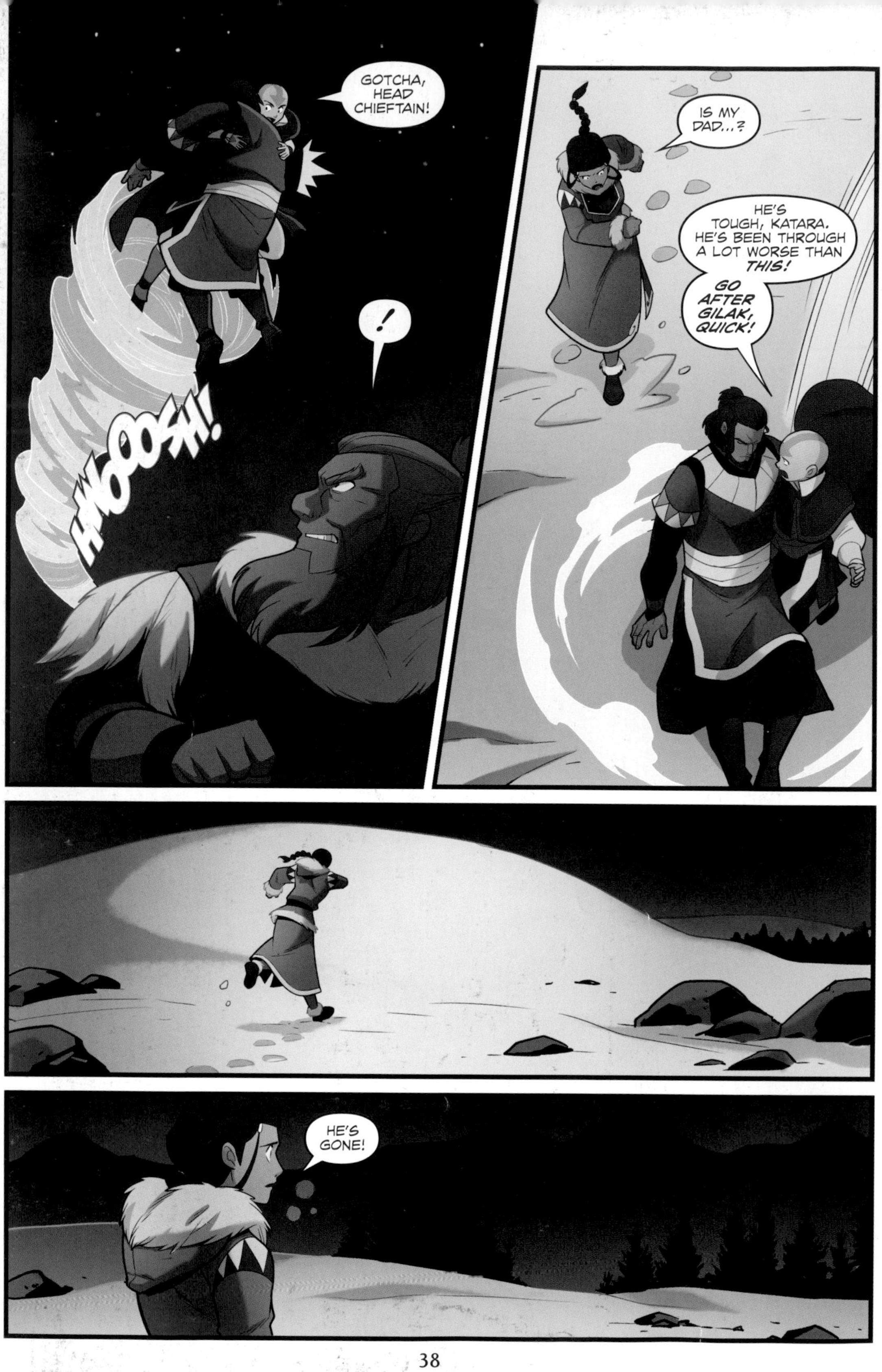
GOTCHA, HEAD CHIEFTAIN!
!
WHOOOSH!
IS MY DAD...?
HE'S TOUGH, KATARA. HE'S BEEN THROUGH A LOT WORSE THAN THIS!
GO AFTER GILAK, QUICK!
HE'S GONE!

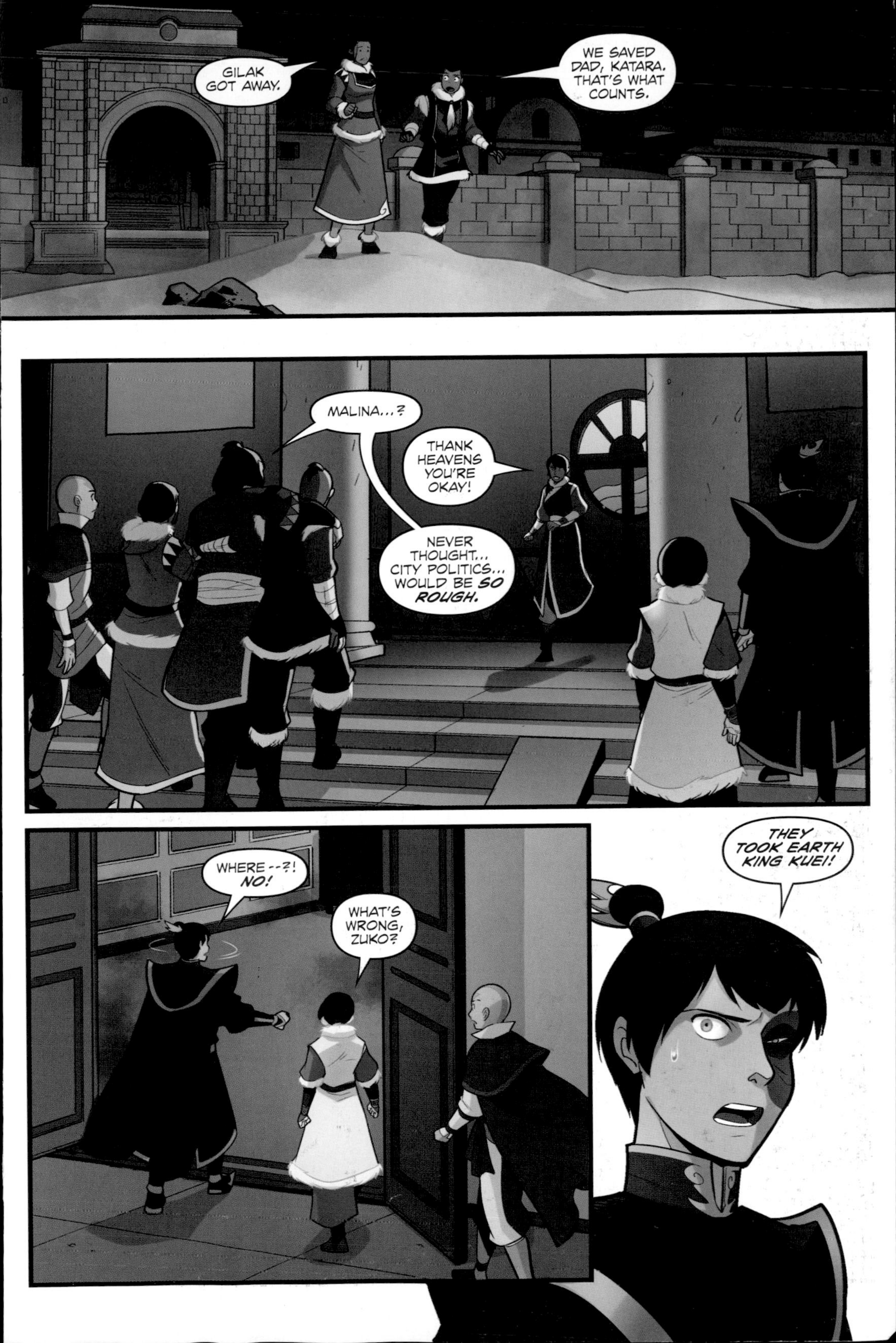
GILAK GOT AWAY.
WE SAVED DAD, KATARA. THAT'S WHAT COUNTS.
MALINA...?
THANK HEAVENS YOU'RE OKAY!
NEVER THOUGHT... CITY POLITICS... WOULD BE SO ROUGH.
WHERE--?! NO!
WHAT'S WRONG, ZUKO?
THEY TOOK EARTH KING KUEI!

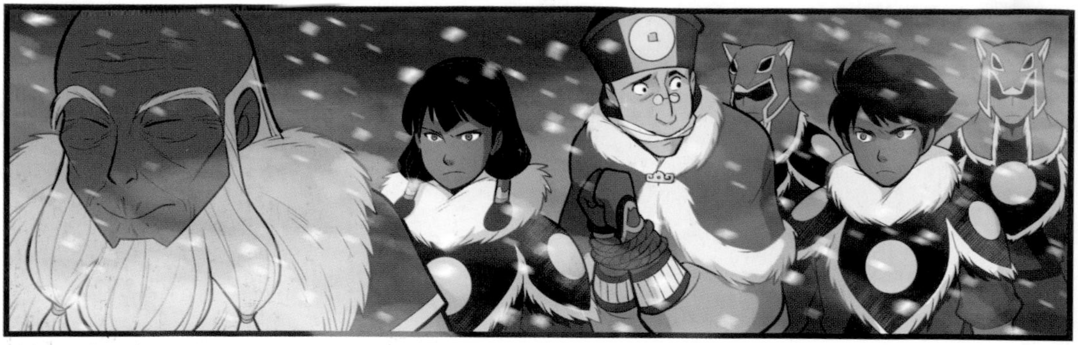

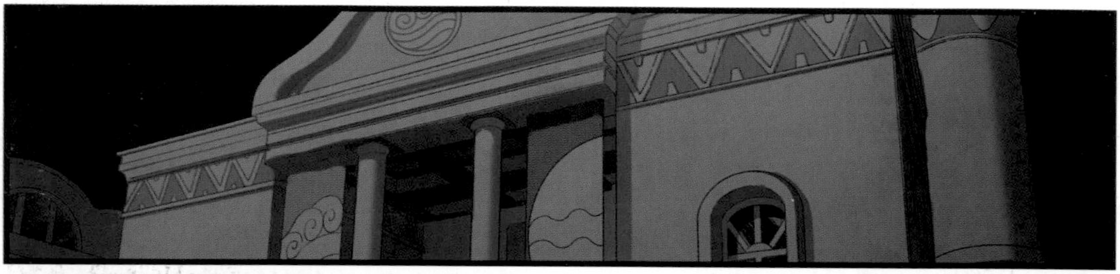

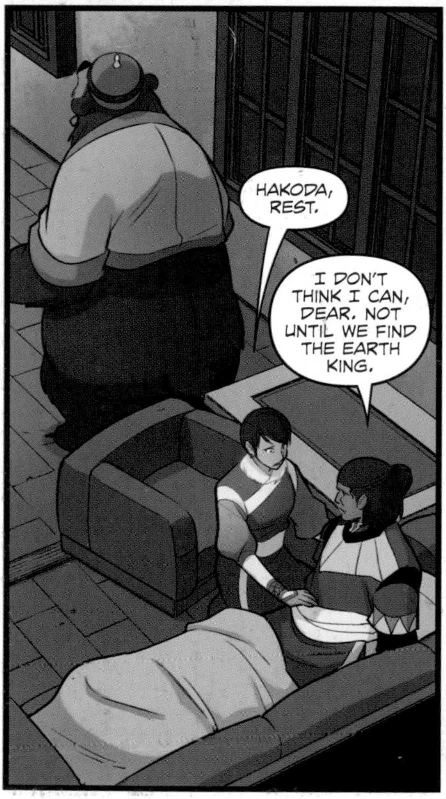
HAKODA, REST.
I DON'T THINK I CAN, DEAR. NOT UNTIL WE FIND THE EARTH KING.

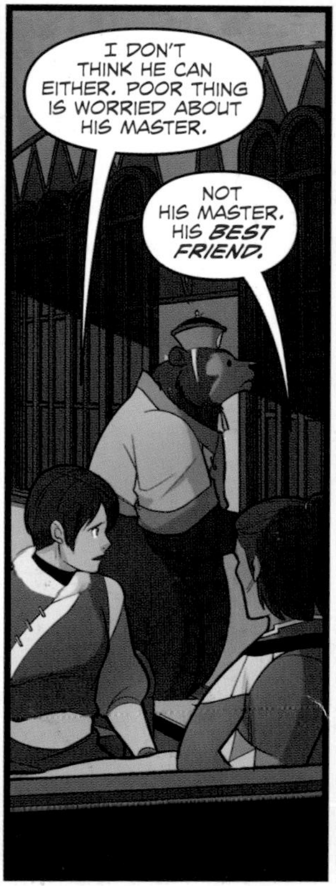
I DON'T THINK HE CAN EITHER. POOR THING IS WORRIED ABOUT HIS MASTER.
NOT HIS MASTER. HIS ***BEST FRIEND.***

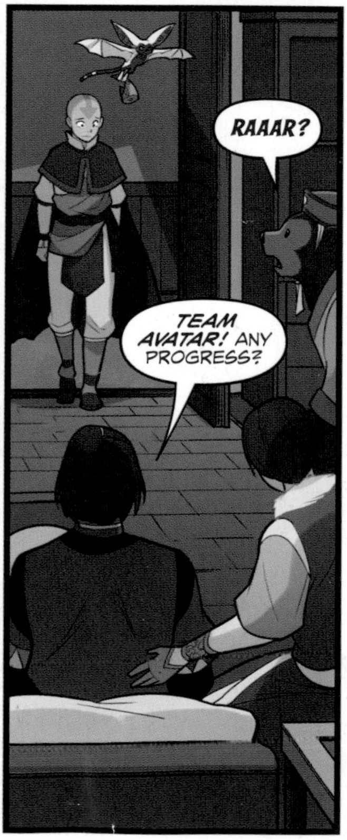
RAAAR?
TEAM AVATAR! ANY PROGRESS?

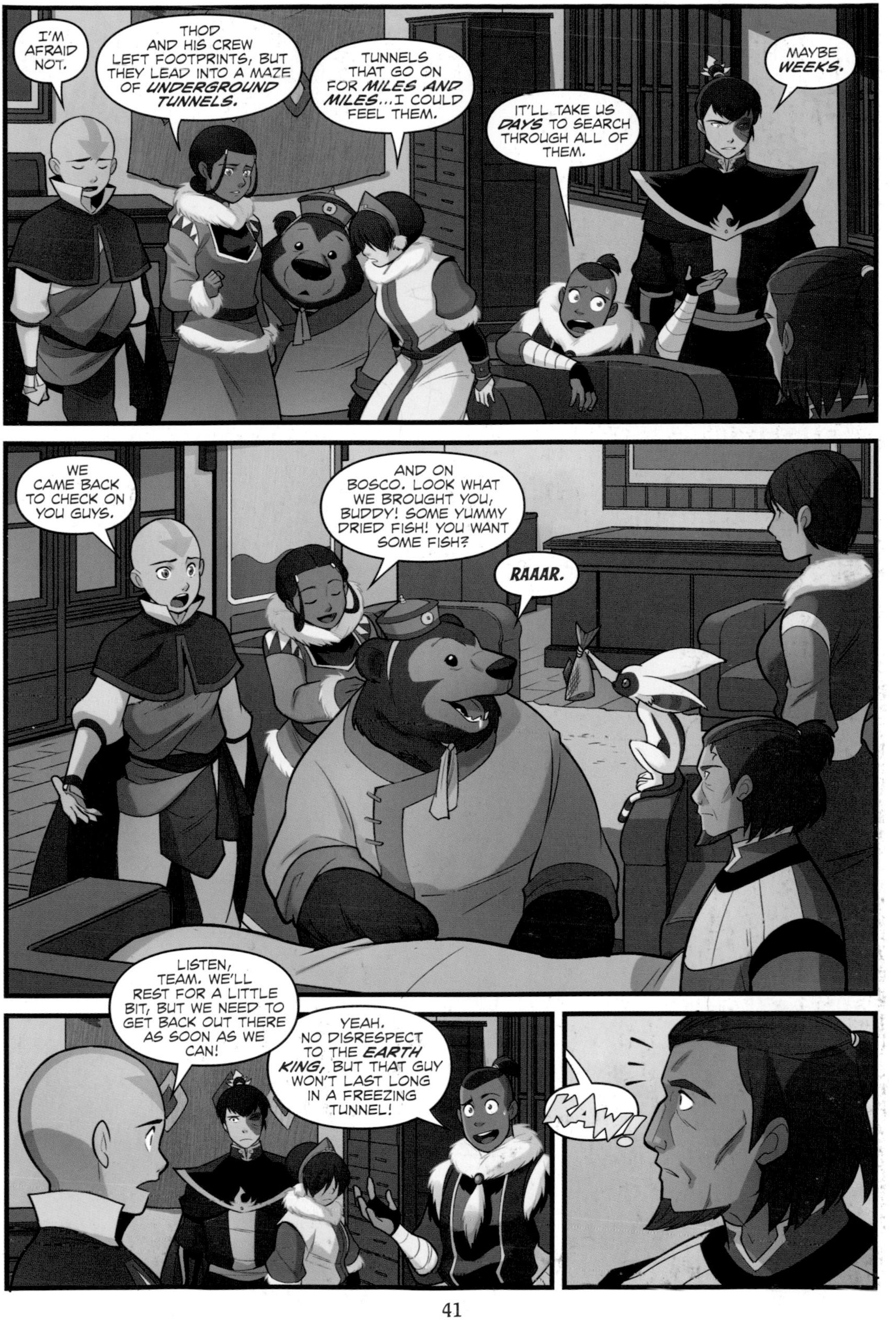
I'M AFRAID NOT.
THOD AND HIS CREW LEFT FOOTPRINTS, BUT THEY LEAD INTO A MAZE OF UNDERGROUND TUNNELS.
TUNNELS THAT GO ON FOR MILES AND MILES...I COULD FEEL THEM.
IT'LL TAKE US DAYS TO SEARCH THROUGH ALL OF THEM.
MAYBE WEEKS.
WE CAME BACK TO CHECK ON YOU GUYS.
AND ON BOSCO. LOOK WHAT WE BROUGHT YOU, BUDDY! SOME YUMMY DRIED FISH! YOU WANT SOME FISH?
RAAAR.
LISTEN, TEAM. WE'LL REST FOR A LITTLE BIT, BUT WE NEED TO GET BACK OUT THERE AS SOON AS WE CAN!
YEAH. NO DISRESPECT TO THE EARTH KING, BUT THAT GUY WON'T LAST LONG IN A FREEZING TUNNEL!
KAW!

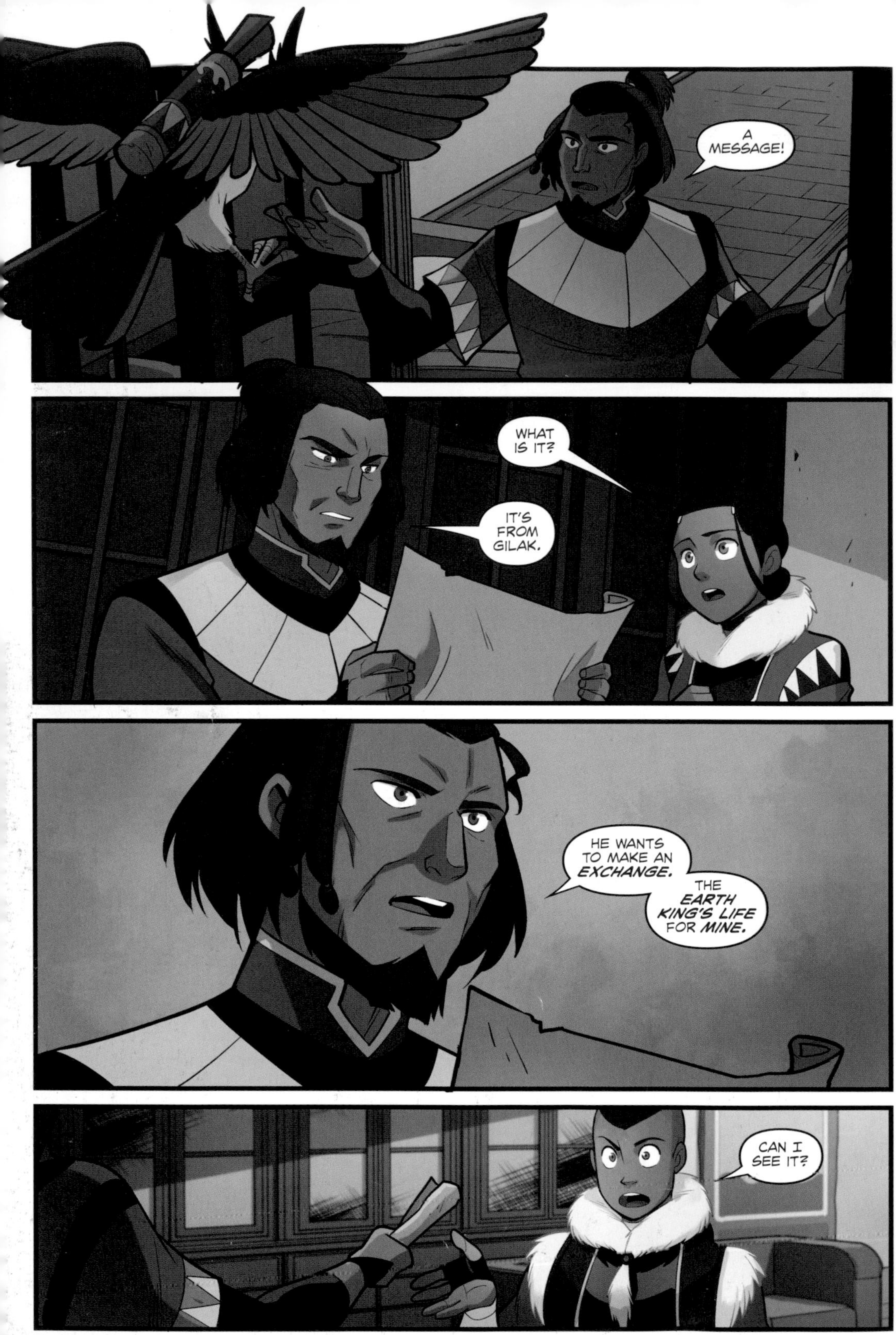
A MESSAGE!
WHAT IS IT?
IT'S FROM GILAK.
HE WANTS TO MAKE AN EXCHANGE.
THE EARTH KING'S LIFE FOR MINE.
CAN I SEE IT?

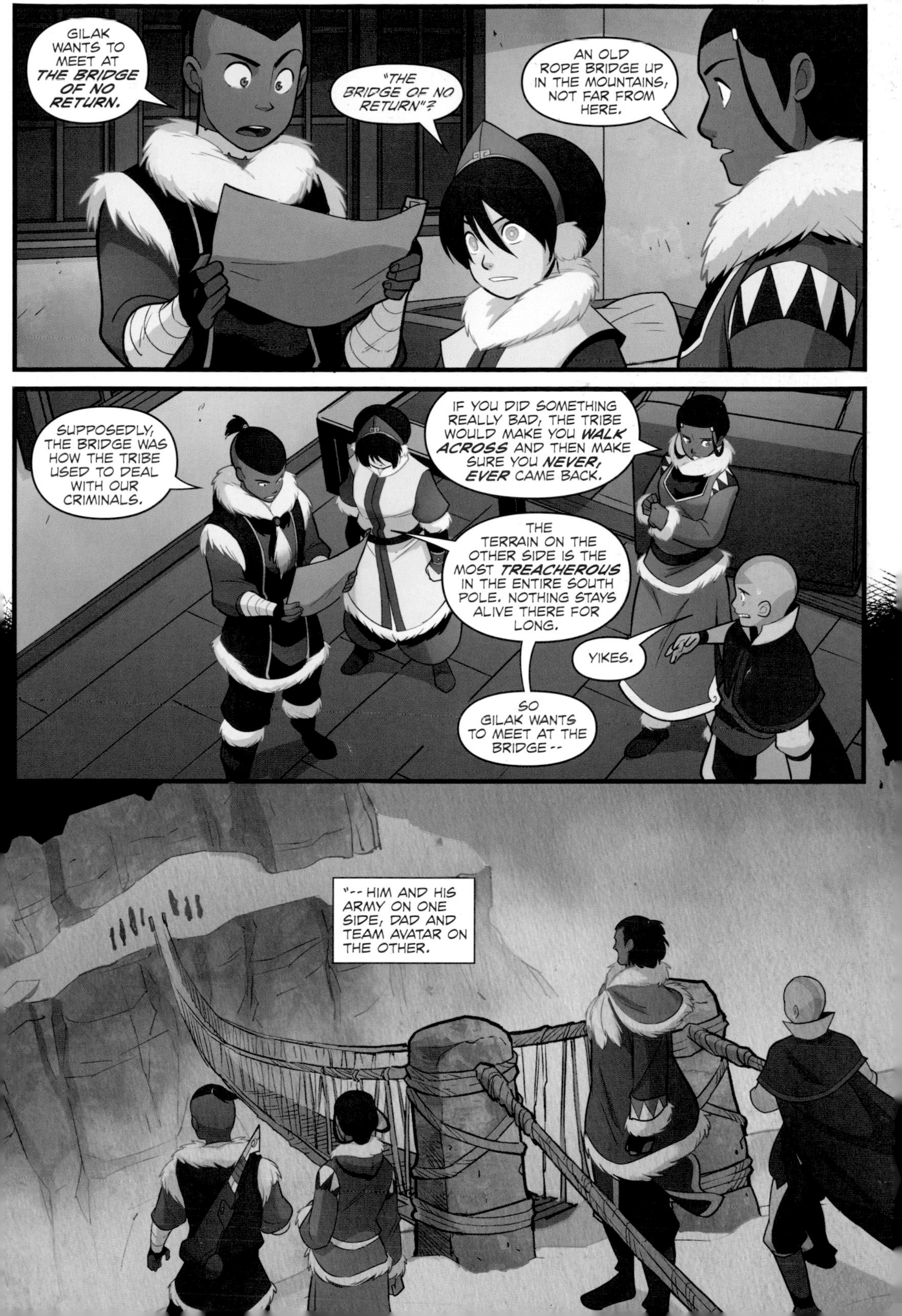
GILAK WANTS TO MEET AT **THE BRIDGE OF NO RETURN.**
"THE BRIDGE OF NO RETURN"?
AN OLD ROPE BRIDGE UP IN THE MOUNTAINS, NOT FAR FROM HERE.
SUPPOSEDLY, THE BRIDGE WAS HOW THE TRIBE USED TO DEAL WITH OUR CRIMINALS.
IF YOU DID SOMETHING REALLY BAD, THE TRIBE WOULD MAKE YOU **WALK ACROSS** AND THEN MAKE SURE YOU **NEVER, EVER** CAME BACK.
THE TERRAIN ON THE OTHER SIDE IS THE MOST **TREACHEROUS** IN THE ENTIRE SOUTH POLE. NOTHING STAYS ALIVE THERE FOR LONG.
YIKES.
SO GILAK WANTS TO MEET AT THE BRIDGE --
"-- HIM AND HIS ARMY ON ONE SIDE, DAD AND TEAM AVATAR ON THE OTHER.

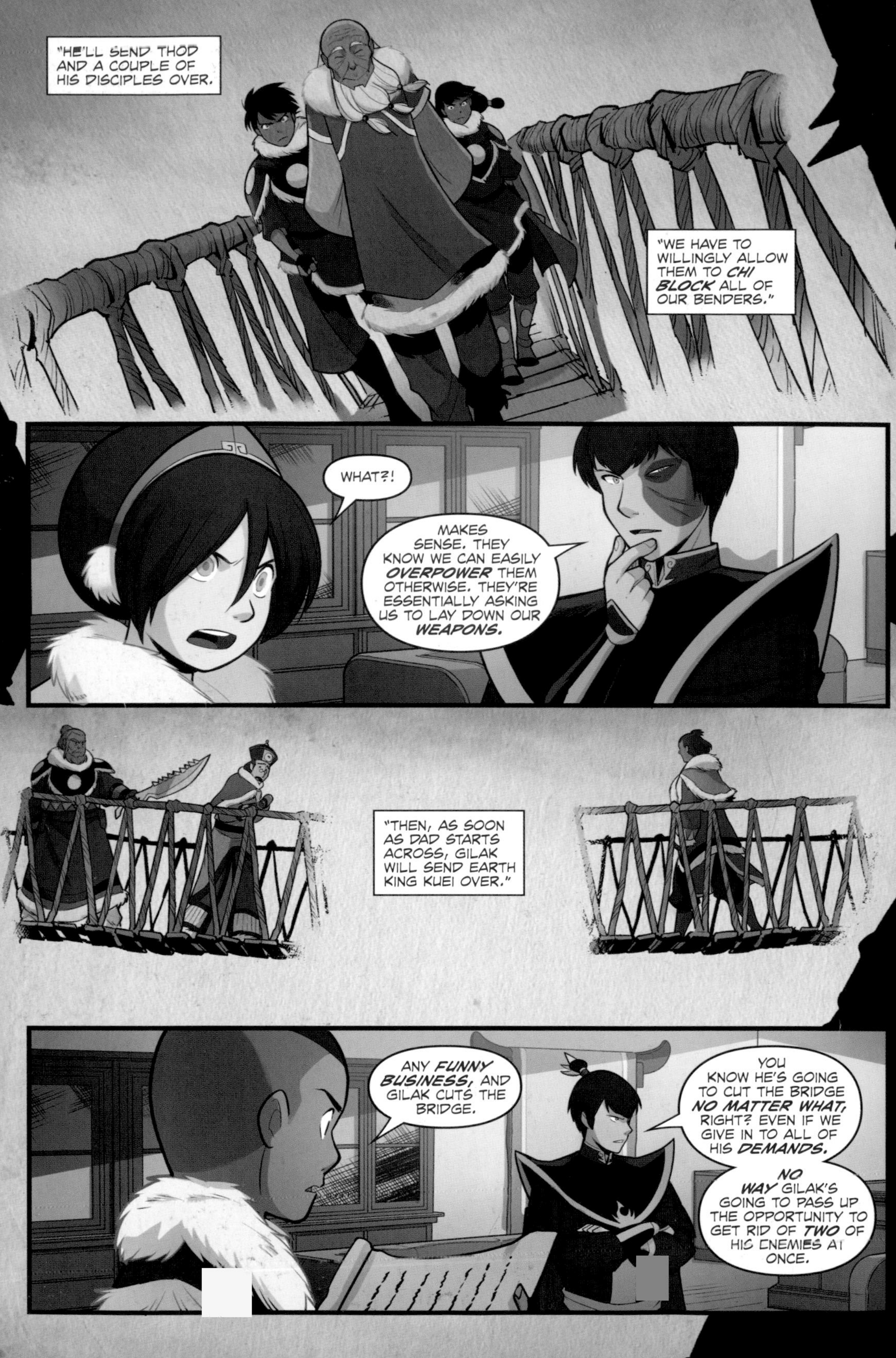
"HE'LL SEND THOD AND A COUPLE OF HIS DISCIPLES OVER.
"WE HAVE TO WILLINGLY ALLOW THEM TO CHI BLOCK ALL OF OUR BENDERS."
WHAT?!
MAKES SENSE. THEY KNOW WE CAN EASILY OVERPOWER THEM OTHERWISE. THEY'RE ESSENTIALLY ASKING US TO LAY DOWN OUR WEAPONS.
"THEN, AS SOON AS DAD STARTS ACROSS, GILAK WILL SEND EARTH KING KUEI OVER."
ANY FUNNY BUSINESS, AND GILAK CUTS THE BRIDGE.
YOU KNOW HE'S GOING TO CUT THE BRIDGE NO MATTER WHAT, RIGHT? EVEN IF WE GIVE IN TO ALL OF HIS DEMANDS.
NO WAY GILAK'S GOING TO PASS UP THE OPPORTUNITY TO GET RID OF TWO OF HIS ENEMIES AT ONCE.

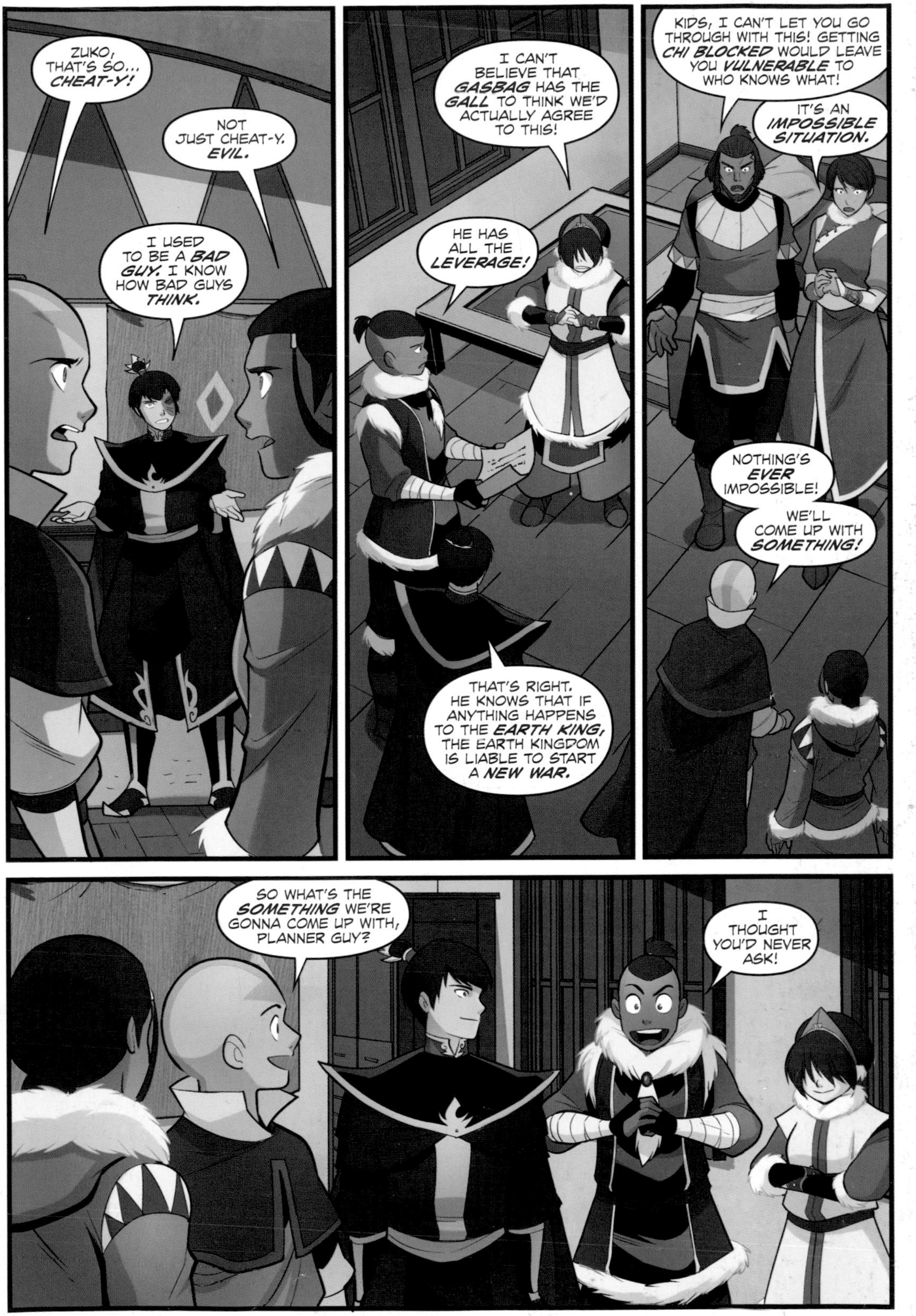
ZUKO, THAT'S SO... CHEAT-Y!
NOT JUST CHEAT-Y. EVIL.
I USED TO BE A BAD GUY. I KNOW HOW BAD GUYS THINK.
I CAN'T BELIEVE THAT GASBAG HAS THE GALL TO THINK WE'D ACTUALLY AGREE TO THIS!
HE HAS ALL THE LEVERAGE!
THAT'S RIGHT. HE KNOWS THAT IF ANYTHING HAPPENS TO THE EARTH KING, THE EARTH KINGDOM IS LIABLE TO START A NEW WAR.
KIDS, I CAN'T LET YOU GO THROUGH WITH THIS! GETTING CHI BLOCKED WOULD LEAVE YOU VULNERABLE TO WHO KNOWS WHAT!
IT'S AN IMPOSSIBLE SITUATION.
NOTHING'S EVER IMPOSSIBLE!
WE'LL COME UP WITH SOMETHING!
SO WHAT'S THE SOMETHING WE'RE GONNA COME UP WITH, PLANNER GUY?
I THOUGHT YOU'D NEVER ASK!

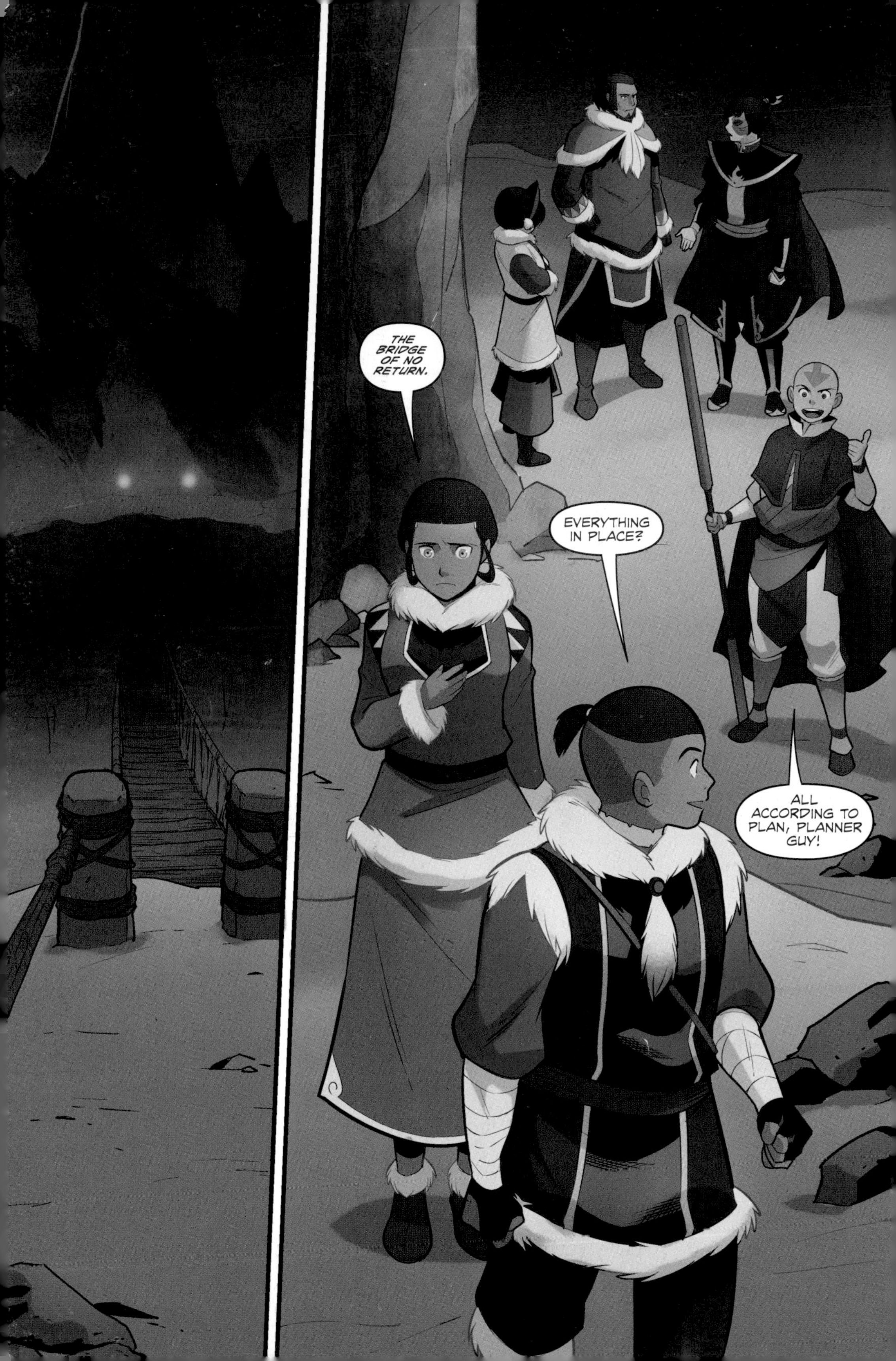
THE BRIDGE OF NO RETURN.
EVERYTHING IN PLACE?
ALL ACCORDING TO PLAN, PLANNER GUY!

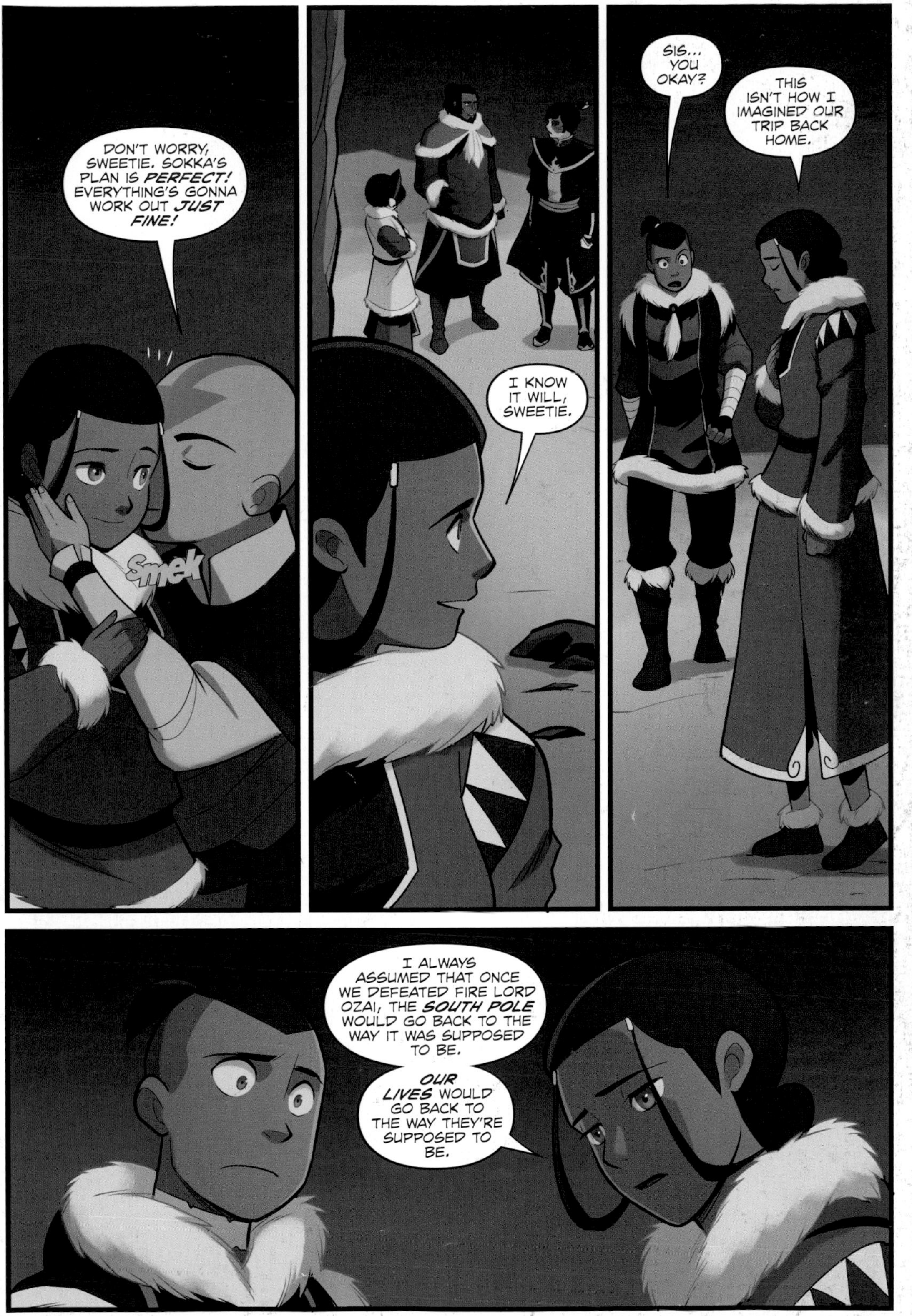
DON'T WORRY, SWEETIE. SOKKA'S PLAN IS PERFECT! EVERYTHING'S GONNA WORK OUT JUST FINE!
Smek
I KNOW IT WILL, SWEETIE.
SIS... YOU OKAY?
THIS ISN'T HOW I IMAGINED OUR TRIP BACK HOME.
I ALWAYS ASSUMED THAT ONCE WE DEFEATED FIRE LORD OZAI, THE SOUTH POLE WOULD GO BACK TO THE WAY IT WAS SUPPOSED TO BE.
OUR LIVES WOULD GO BACK TO THE WAY THEY'RE SUPPOSED TO BE.

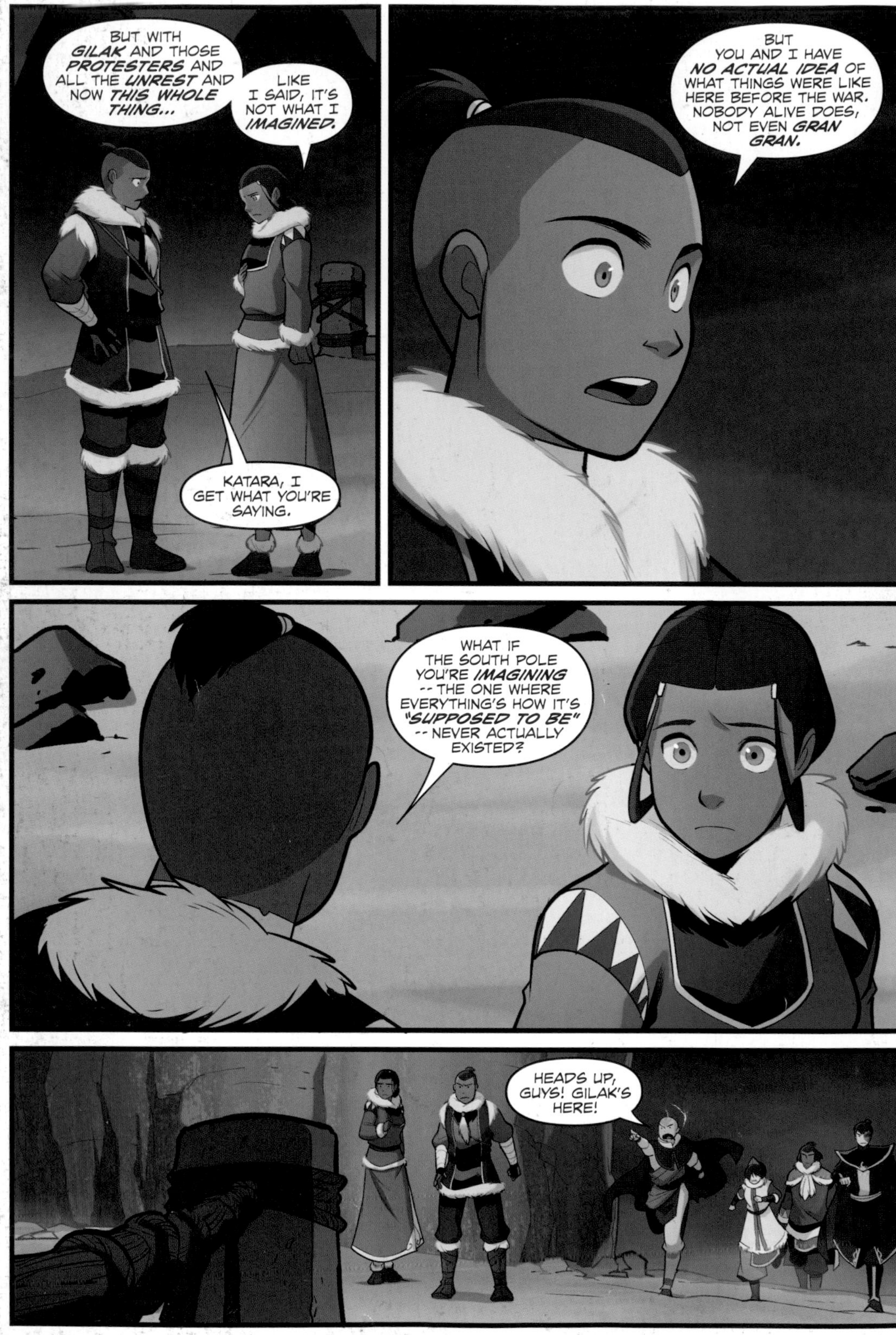
BUT WITH GILAK AND THOSE PROTESTERS AND ALL THE UNREST AND NOW THIS WHOLE THING...
LIKE I SAID, IT'S NOT WHAT I IMAGINED.
KATARA, I GET WHAT YOU'RE SAYING.
BUT YOU AND I HAVE NO ACTUAL IDEA OF WHAT THINGS WERE LIKE HERE BEFORE THE WAR. NOBODY ALIVE DOES, NOT EVEN GRAN GRAN.
WHAT IF THE SOUTH POLE YOU'RE IMAGINING -- THE ONE WHERE EVERYTHING'S HOW IT'S "SUPPOSED TO BE" -- NEVER ACTUALLY EXISTED?
HEADS UP, GUYS! GILAK'S HERE!

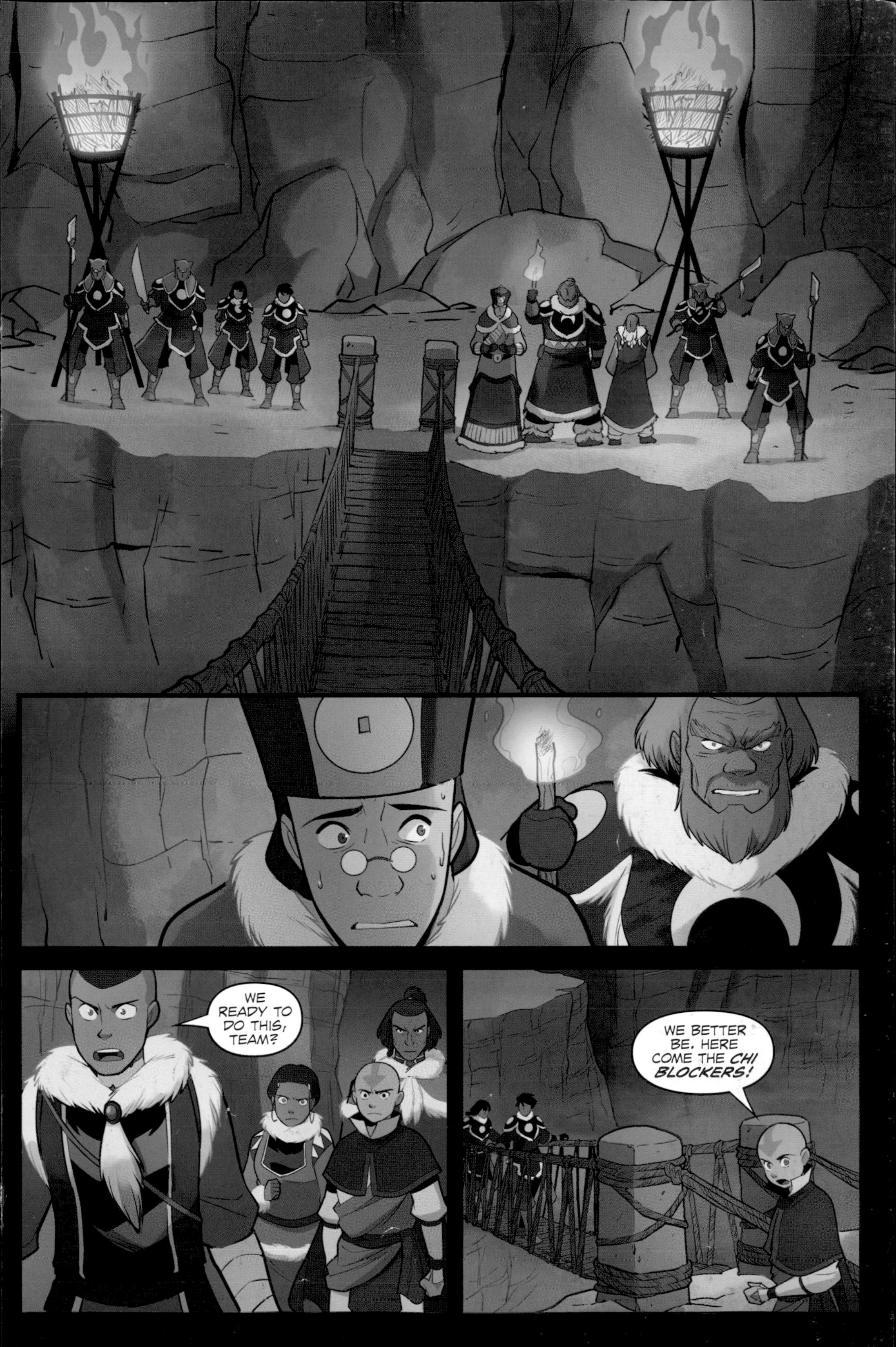
WE READY TO DO THIS, TEAM?
WE BETTER BE. HERE COME THE *CHI BLOCKERS!*

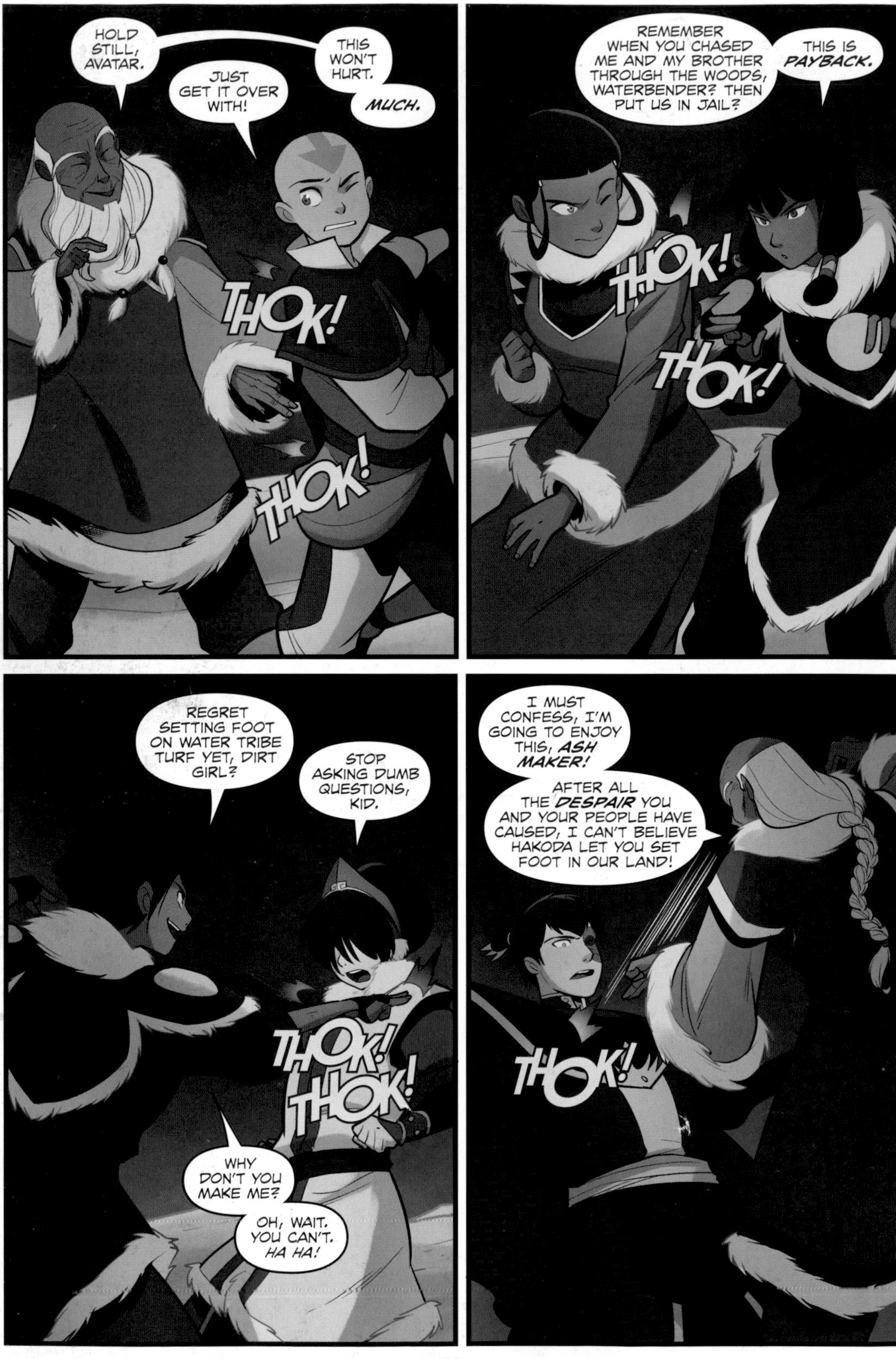
HOLD STILL, AVATAR.
THIS WON'T HURT.
JUST GET IT OVER WITH!
MUCH.
THOK!
THOK!
REMEMBER WHEN YOU CHASED ME AND MY BROTHER THROUGH THE WOODS, WATERBENDER? THEN PUT US IN JAIL?
THIS IS PAYBACK.
THOK!
THOK!
REGRET SETTING FOOT ON WATER TRIBE TURF YET, DIRT GIRL?
STOP ASKING DUMB QUESTIONS, KID.
THOK! THOK!
WHY DON'T YOU MAKE ME?
OH, WAIT. YOU CAN'T. HA HA!
I MUST CONFESS, I'M GOING TO ENJOY THIS, ASH MAKER!
AFTER ALL THE DESPAIR YOU AND YOUR PEOPLE HAVE CAUSED, I CAN'T BELIEVE HAKODA LET YOU SET FOOT IN OUR LAND!
THOK!

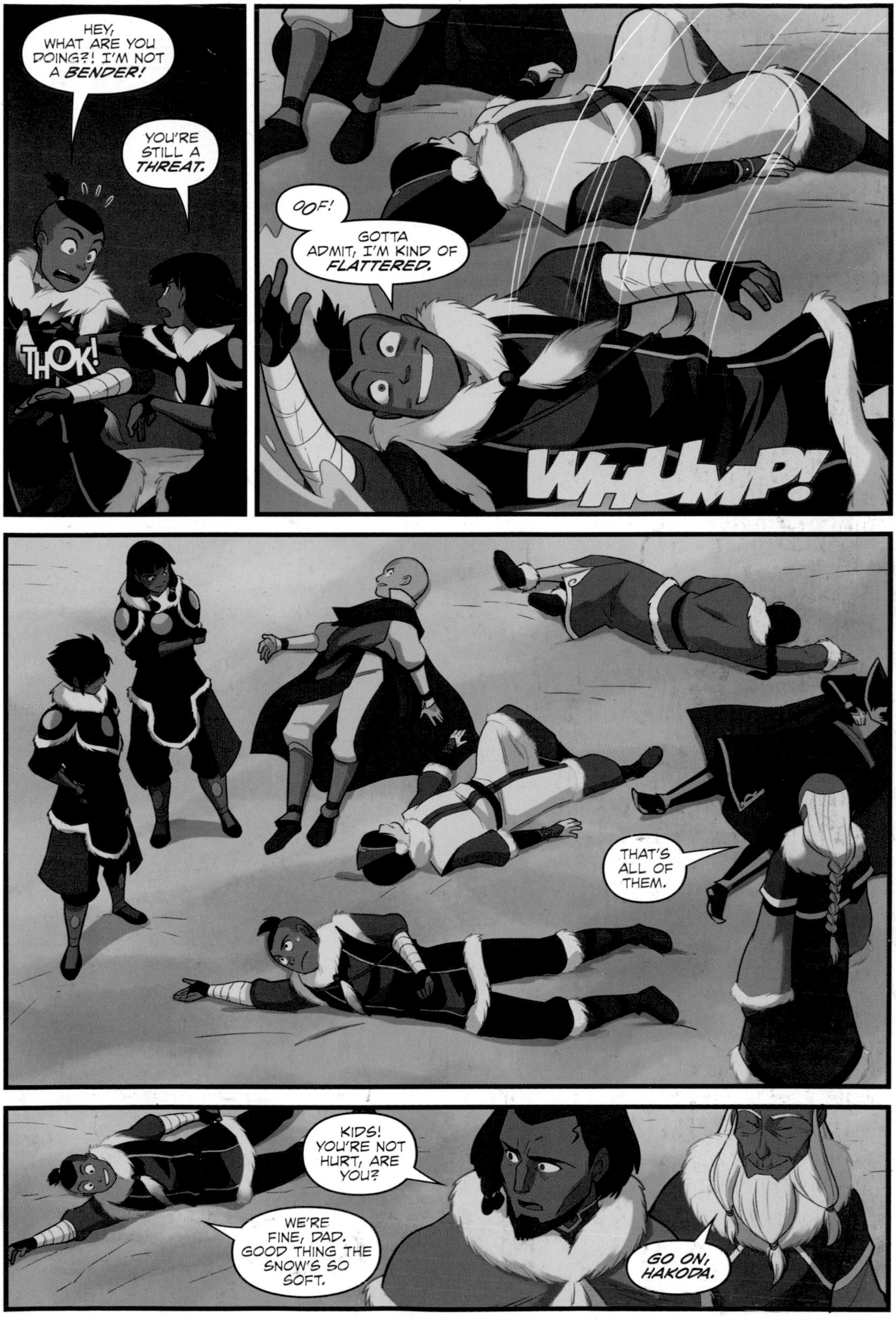
HEY, WHAT ARE YOU DOING?! I'M NOT A BENDER!
YOU'RE STILL A THREAT.
THOK!
OOF!
GOTTA ADMIT, I'M KIND OF FLATTERED.
WHUMP!
THAT'S ALL OF THEM.
KIDS! YOU'RE NOT HURT, ARE YOU?
WE'RE FINE, DAD. GOOD THING THE SNOW'S SO SOFT.
GO ON, HAKODA.

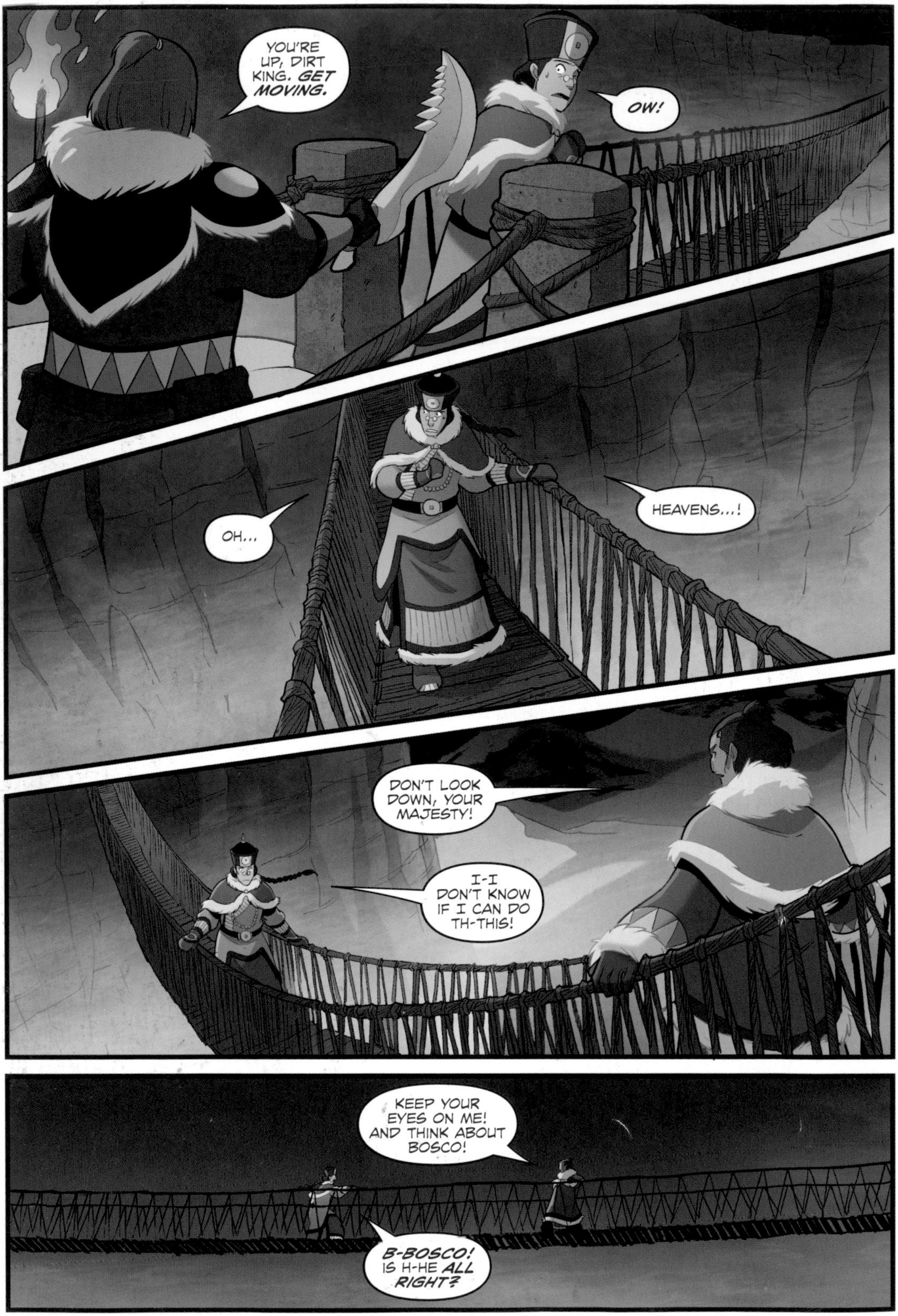
YOU'RE UP, DIRT KING. GET MOVING.
OW!
OH...
HEAVENS...!
DON'T LOOK DOWN, YOUR MAJESTY!
I-I DON'T KNOW IF I CAN DO TH-THIS!
KEEP YOUR EYES ON ME! AND THINK ABOUT BOSCO!
B-BOSCO! IS H-HE ALL RIGHT?

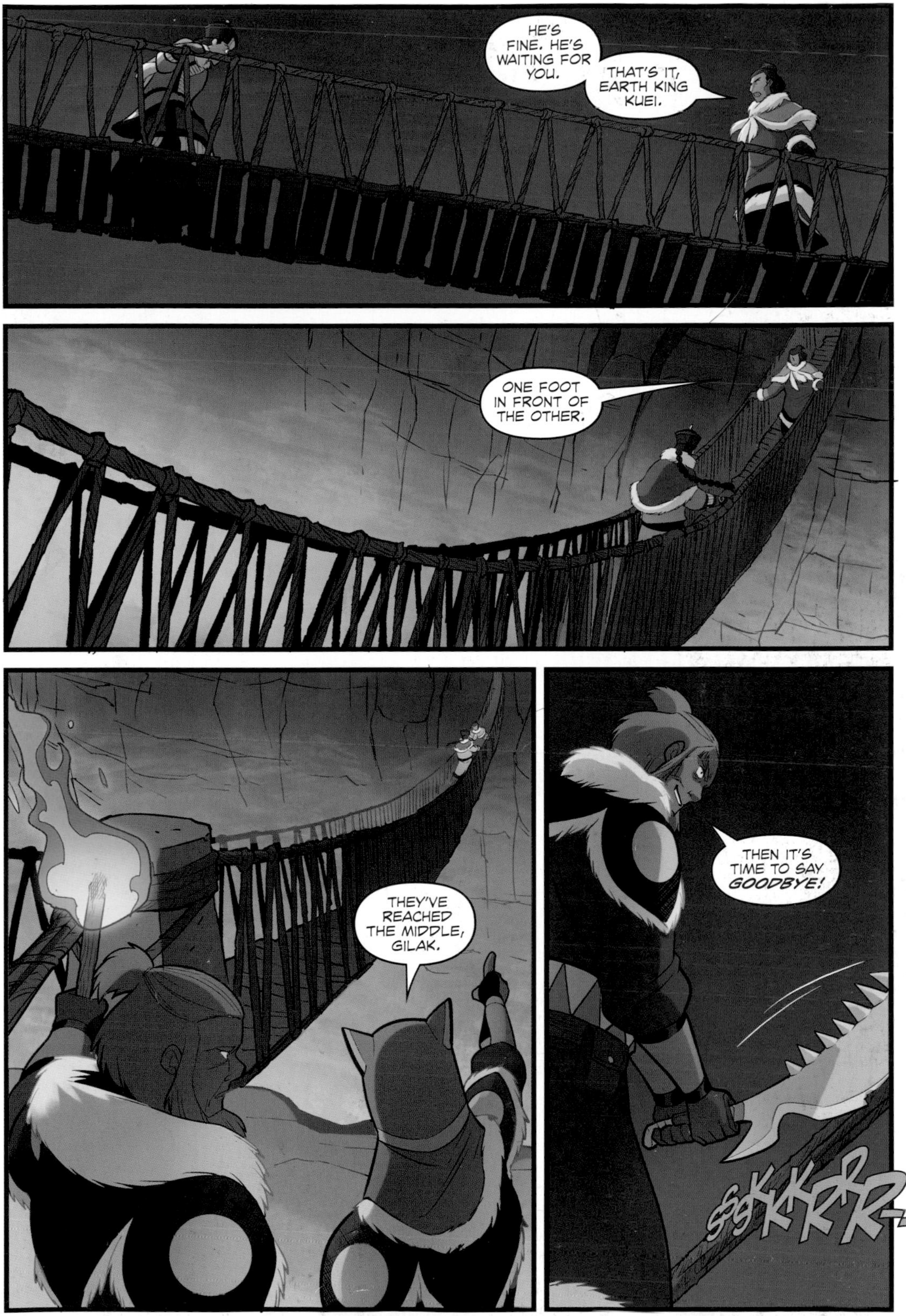
HE'S FINE. HE'S WAITING FOR YOU.
THAT'S IT, EARTH KING KUEI.
ONE FOOT IN FRONT OF THE OTHER.
THEY'VE REACHED THE MIDDLE, GILAK.
THEN IT'S TIME TO SAY *GOODBYE!*
SSGKKKRR-

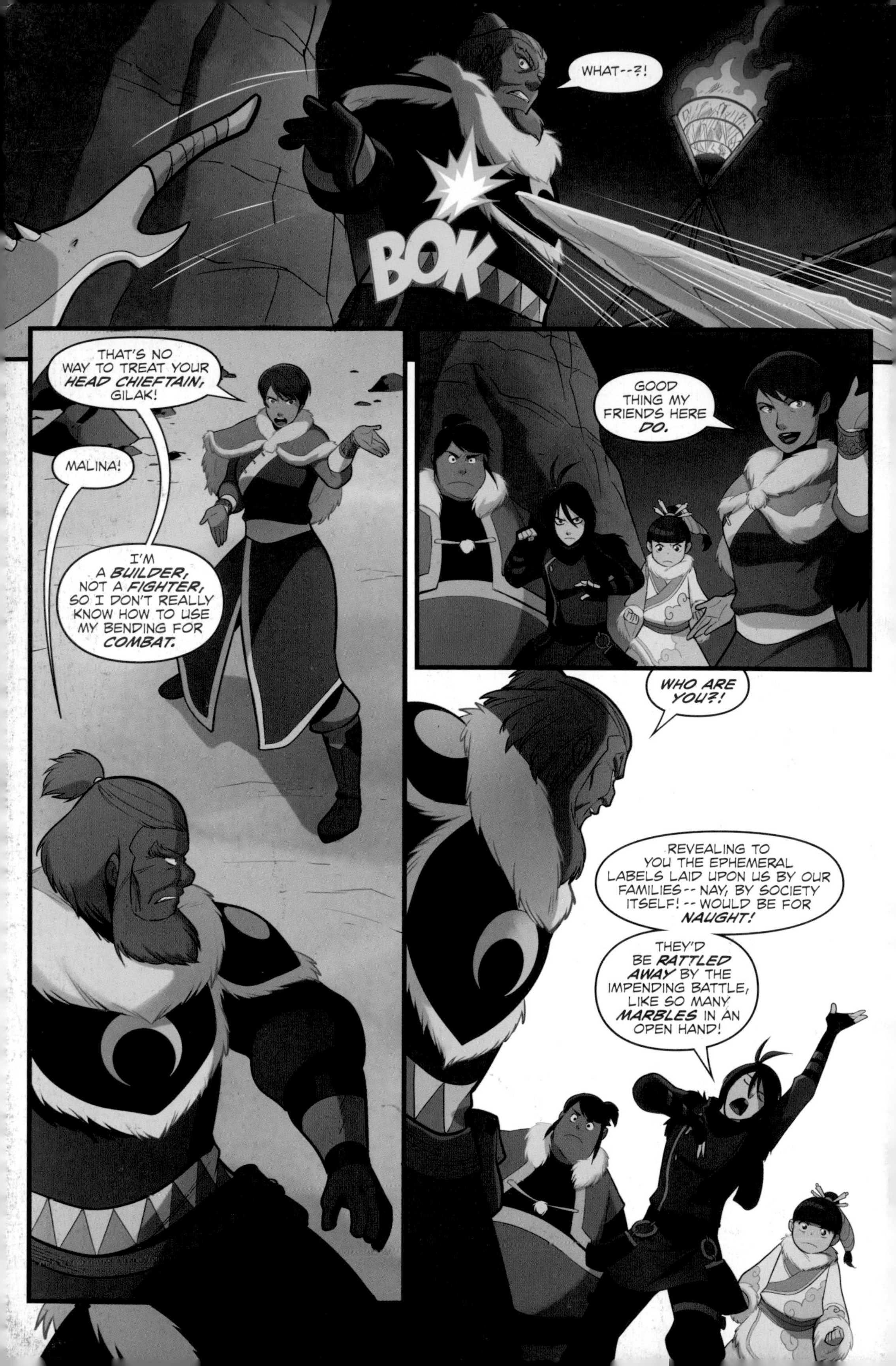
WHAT--?!
BOK
THAT'S NO WAY TO TREAT YOUR *HEAD CHIEFTAIN,* GILAK!
MALINA!
I'M A *BUILDER,* NOT A *FIGHTER,* SO I DON'T REALLY KNOW HOW TO USE MY BENDING FOR *COMBAT.*
GOOD THING MY FRIENDS HERE *DO.*
WHO ARE YOU?!
REVEALING TO YOU THE EPHEMERAL LABELS LAID UPON US BY OUR FAMILIES-- NAY, BY SOCIETY ITSELF! --WOULD BE FOR *NAUGHT!*
THEY'D BE *RATTLED AWAY* BY THE IMPENDING BATTLE, LIKE SO MANY *MARBLES* IN AN OPEN HAND!

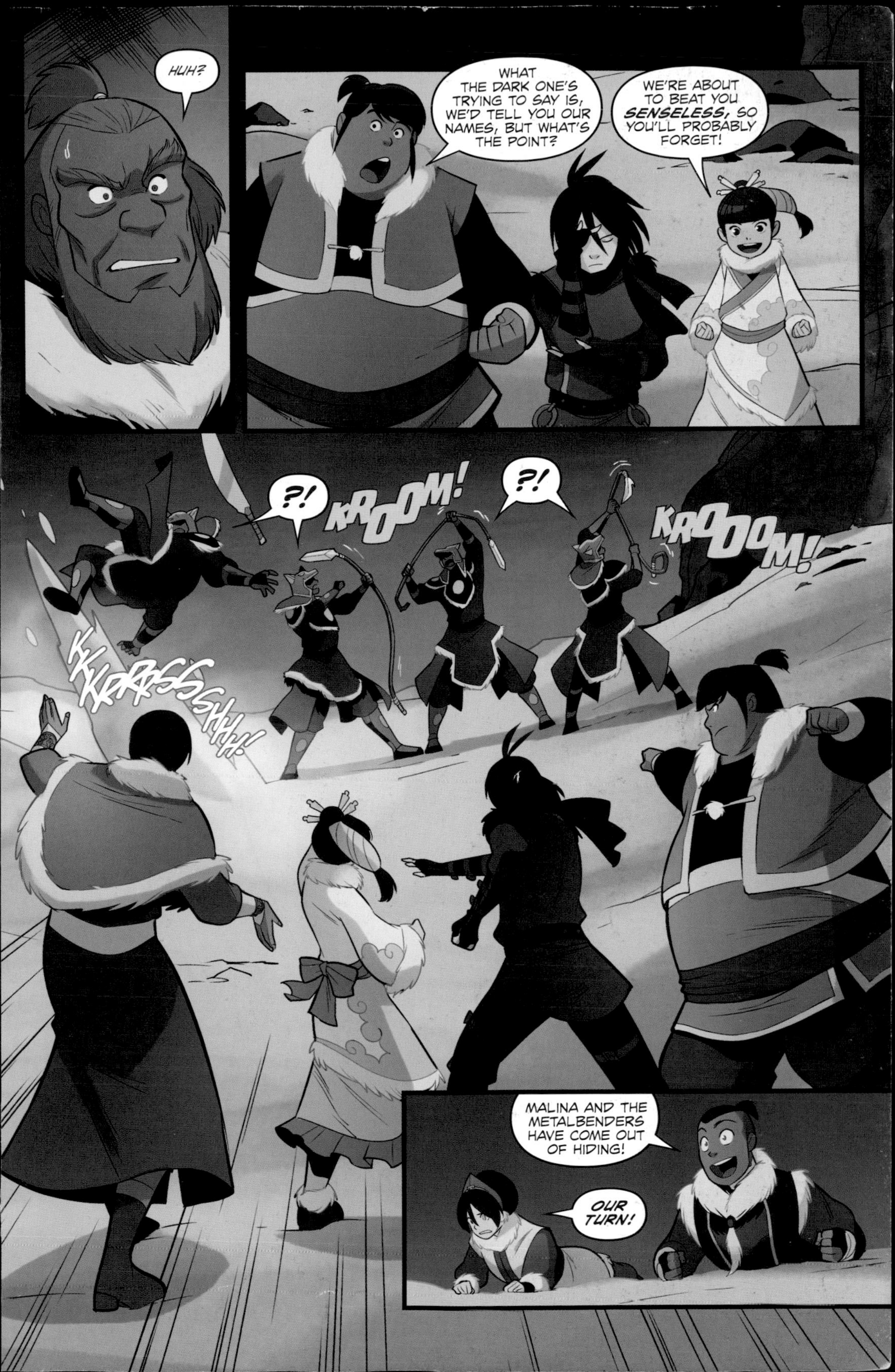
HUH?
WHAT THE DARK ONE'S TRYING TO SAY IS, WE'D TELL YOU OUR NAMES, BUT WHAT'S THE POINT?
WE'RE ABOUT TO BEAT YOU SENSELESS, SO YOU'LL PROBABLY FORGET!
?!
KROOOM!
?!
KROOOOM!
KKKRRRSSSHHH!
MALINA AND THE METALBENDERS HAVE COME OUT OF HIDING!
OUR TURN!

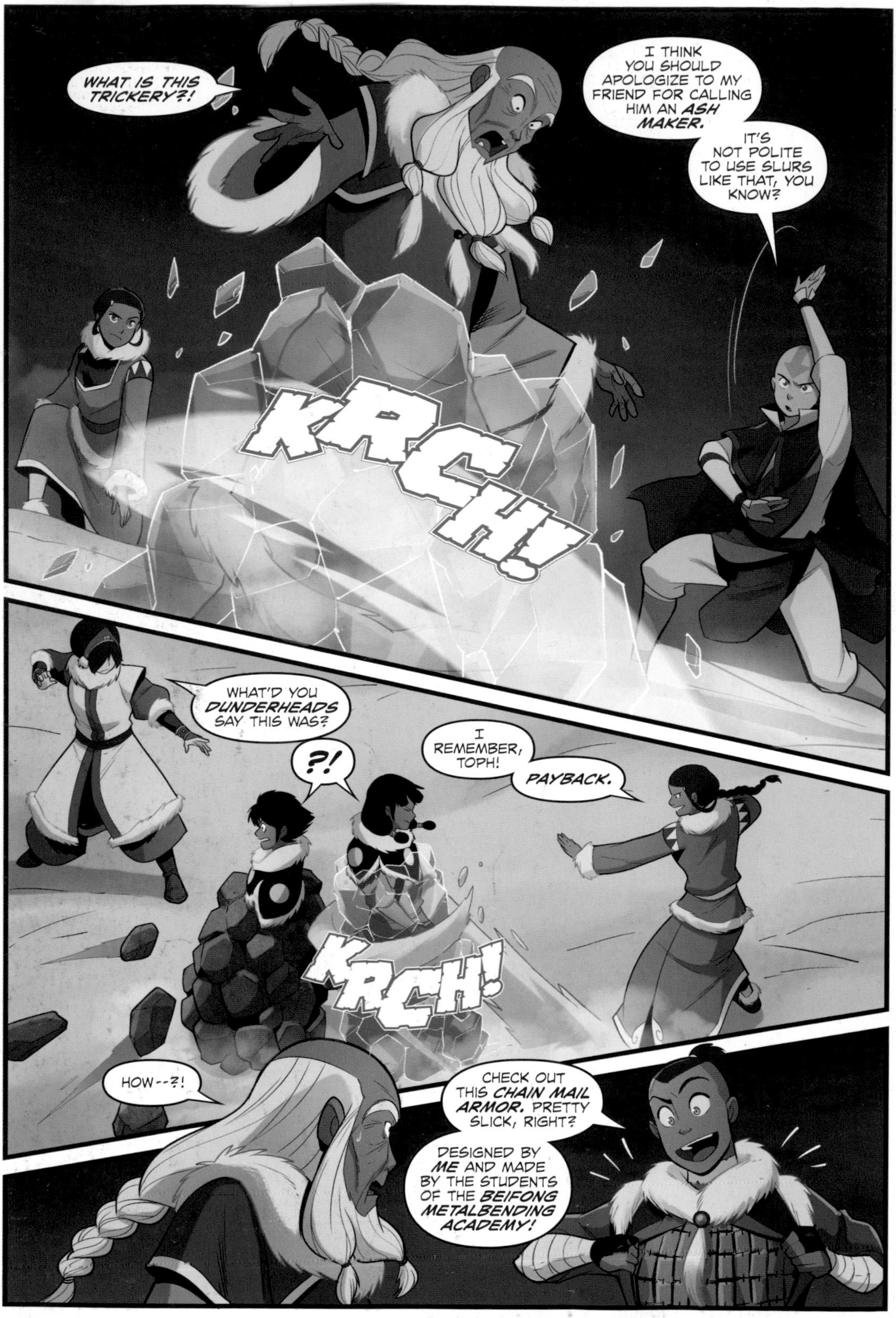
WHAT IS THIS TRICKERY?!
I THINK YOU SHOULD APOLOGIZE TO MY FRIEND FOR CALLING HIM AN ASH MAKER.
IT'S NOT POLITE TO USE SLURS LIKE THAT, YOU KNOW?
KRCH!
WHAT'D YOU DUNDERHEADS SAY THIS WAS?
?!
I REMEMBER, TOPH!
PAYBACK.
KRCH!
HOW--?!
CHECK OUT THIS CHAIN MAIL ARMOR. PRETTY SLICK, RIGHT?
DESIGNED BY ME AND MADE BY THE STUDENTS OF THE BEIFONG METALBENDING ACADEMY!

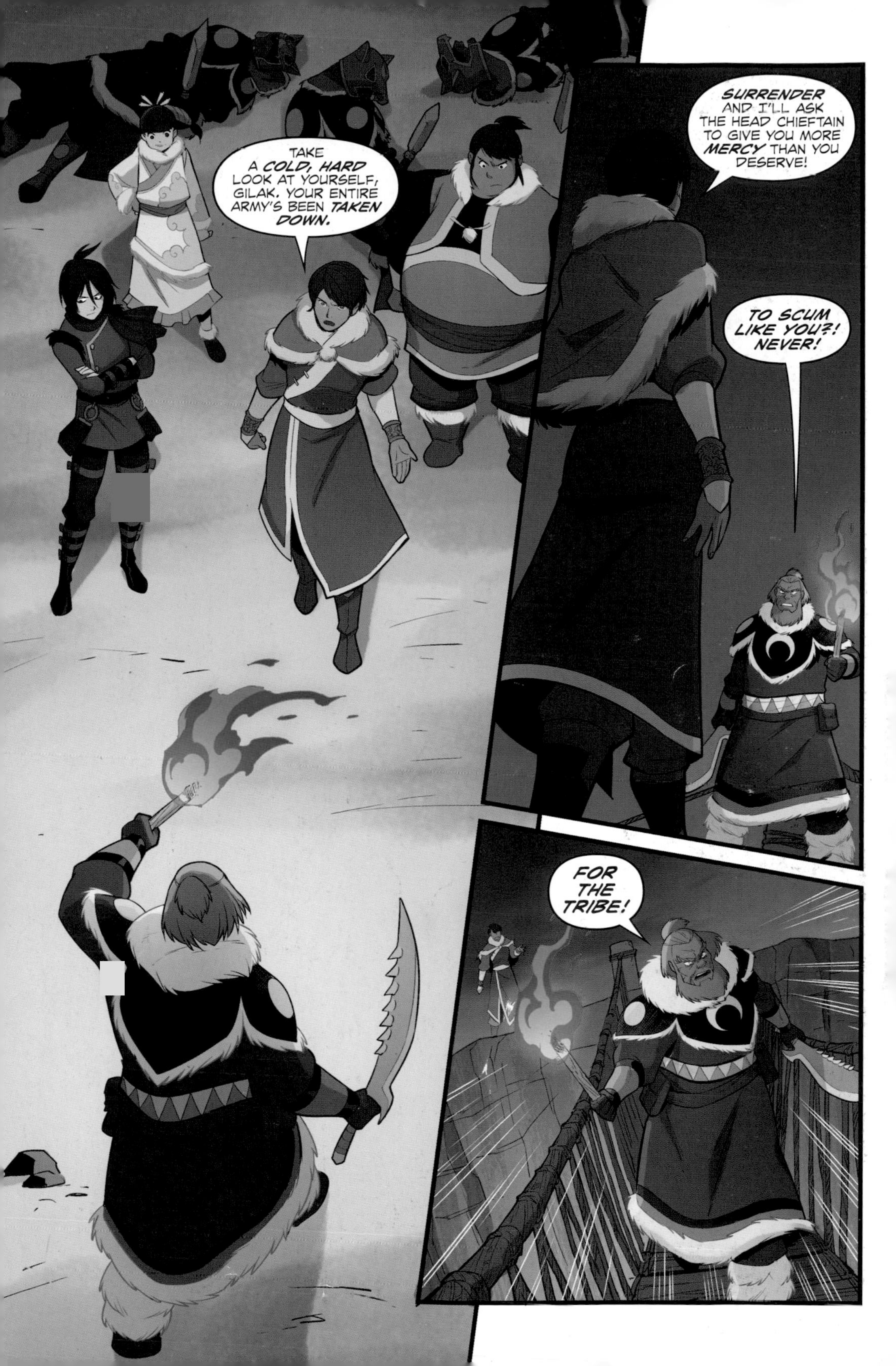

TAKE A COLD, HARD LOOK AT YOURSELF, GILAK. YOUR ENTIRE ARMY'S BEEN TAKEN DOWN.
SURRENDER AND I'LL ASK THE HEAD CHIEFTAIN TO GIVE YOU MORE MERCY THAN YOU DESERVE!
TO SCUM LIKE YOU?! NEVER!
FOR THE TRIBE!

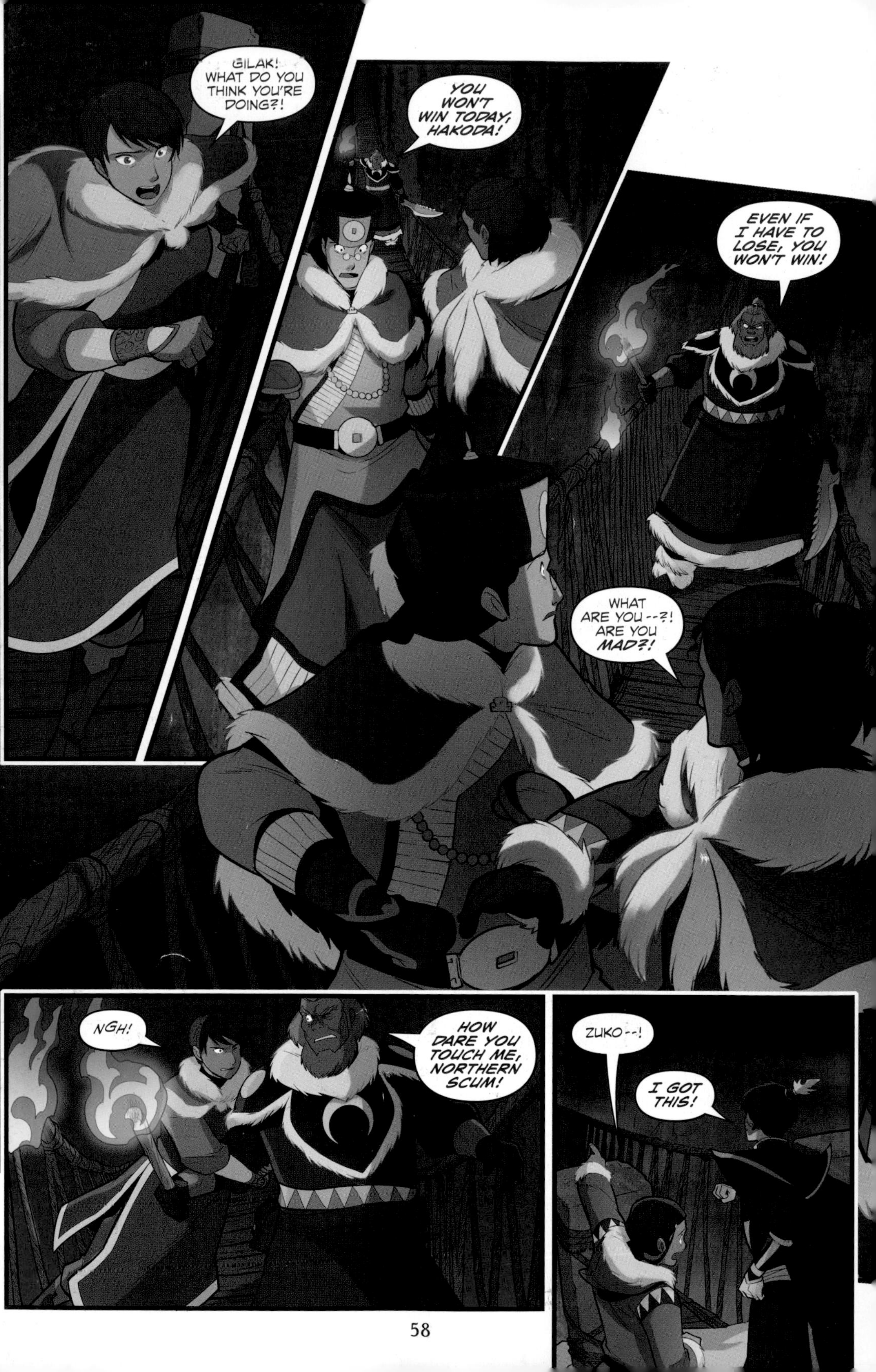
GILAK! WHAT DO YOU THINK YOU'RE DOING?!
YOU WON'T WIN TODAY, HAKODA!
EVEN IF I HAVE TO LOSE, YOU WON'T WIN!
WHAT ARE YOU--?! ARE YOU MAD?!
NGH!
HOW DARE YOU TOUCH ME, NORTHERN SCUM!
ZUKO--!
I GOT THIS!

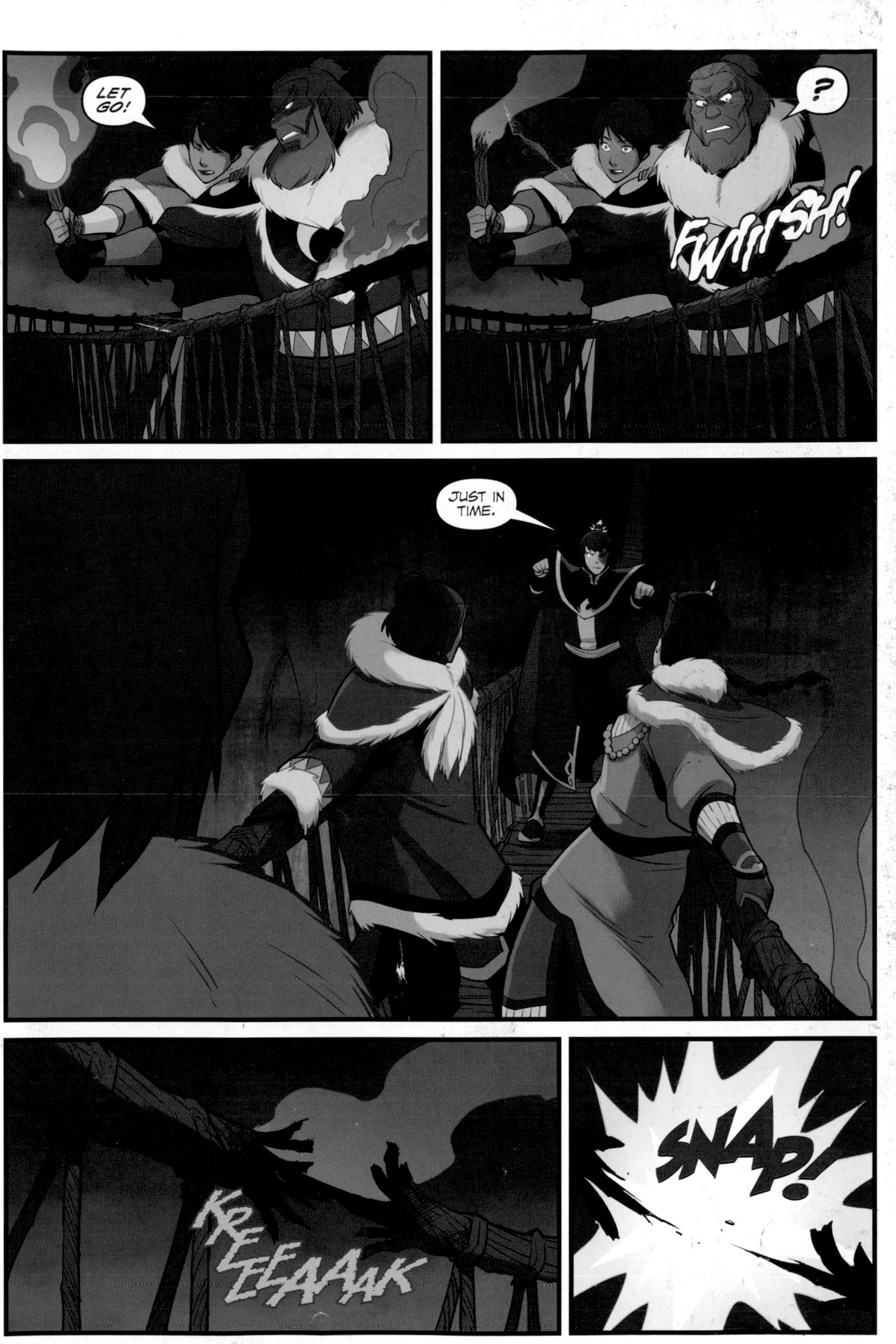
LET GO!
?
FWIIISH!
JUST IN TIME.
KREEEEAAAAK
SNAP!

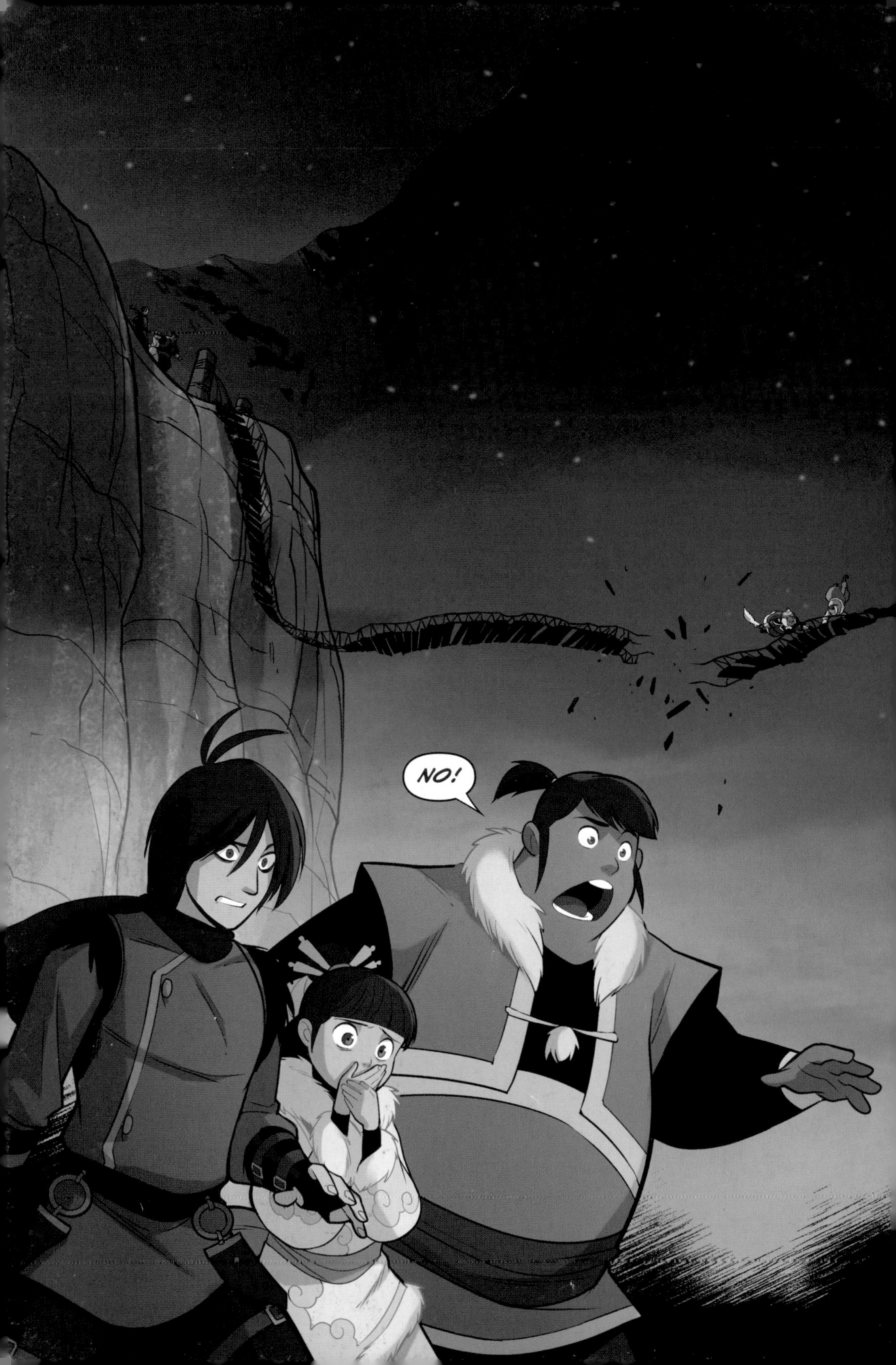
NO!

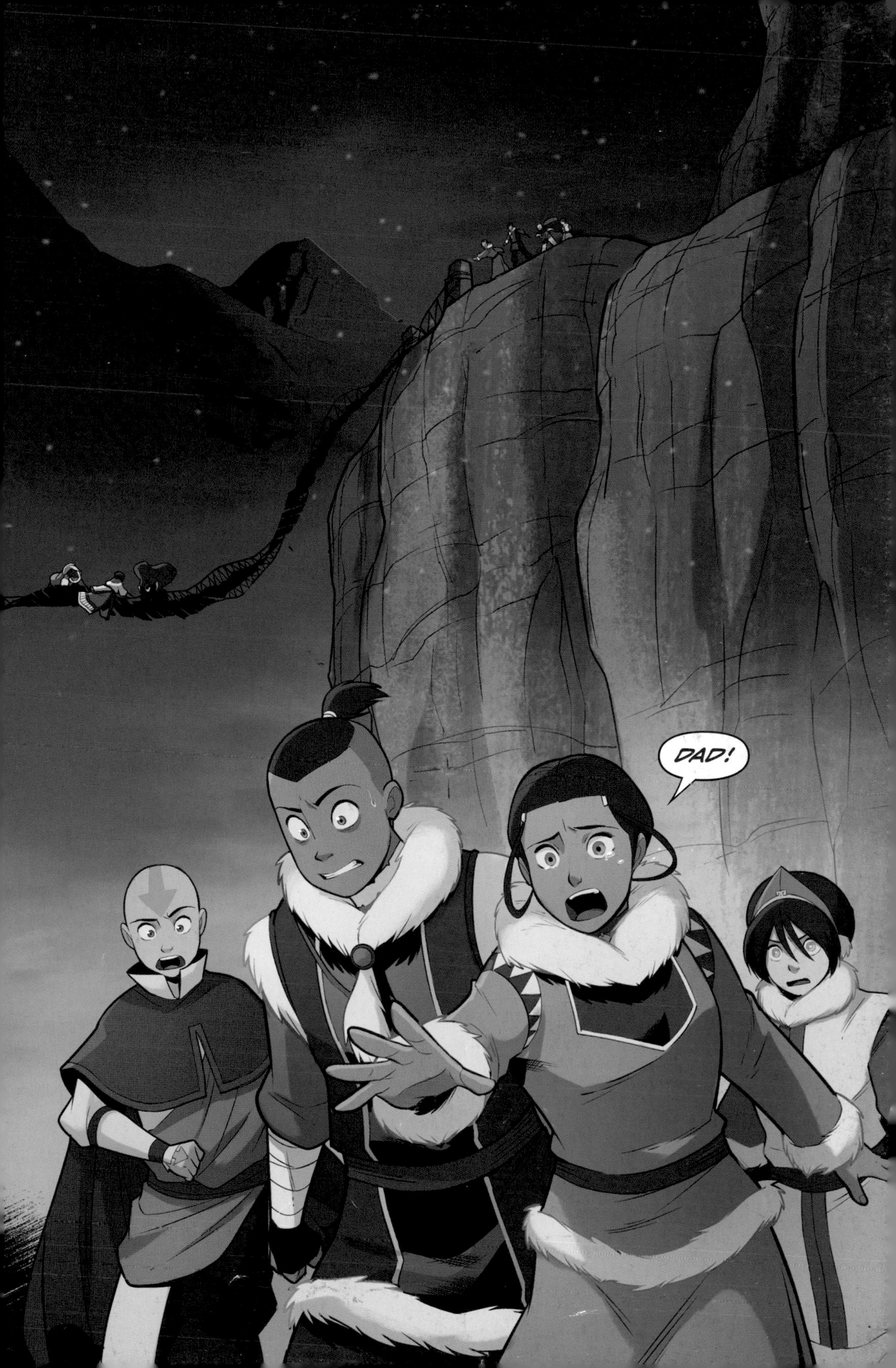
DAD!

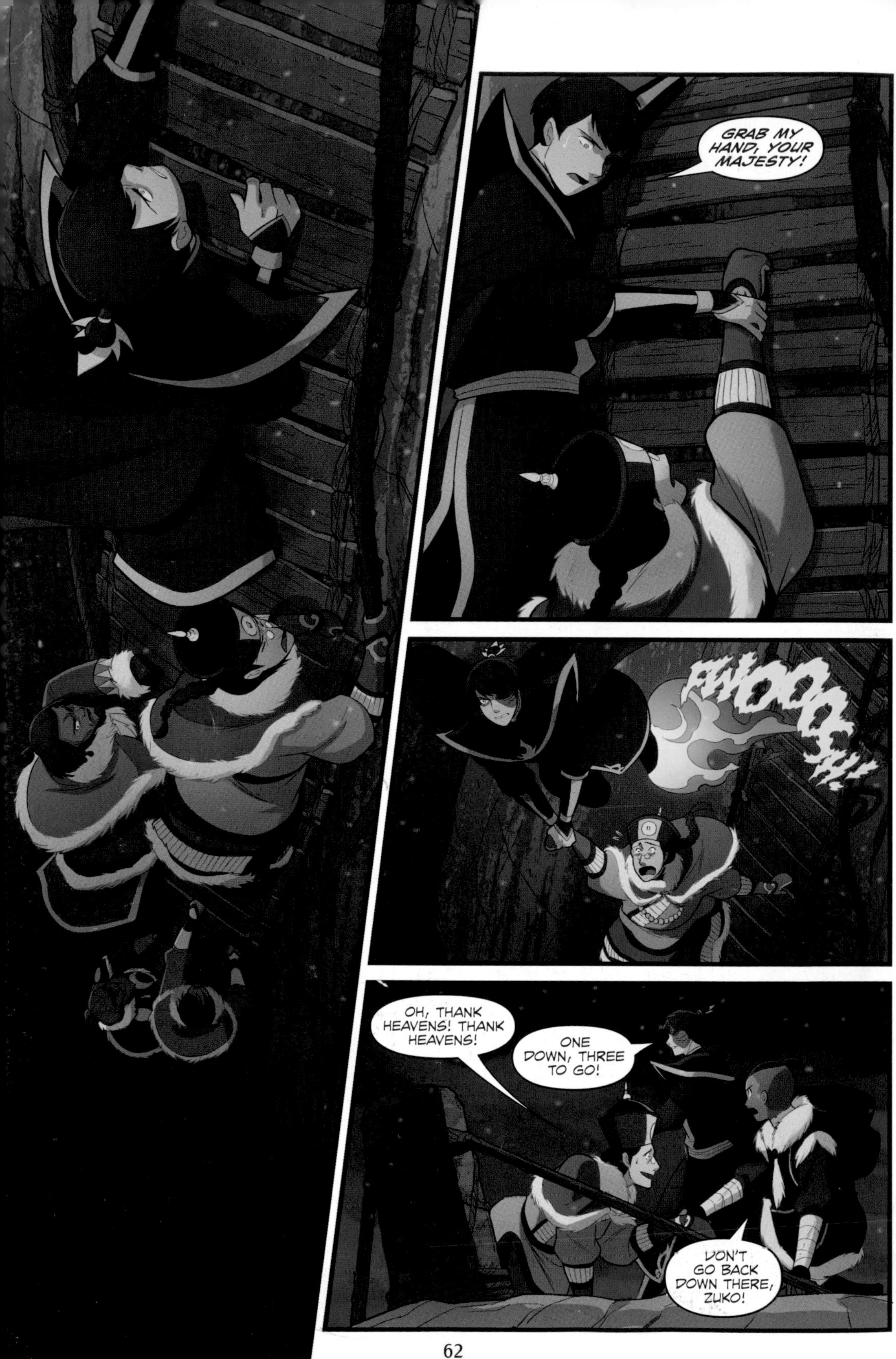
GRAB MY HAND, YOUR MAJESTY!
FWOOSH!
OH, THANK HEAVENS! THANK HEAVENS!
ONE DOWN, THREE TO GO!
DON'T GO BACK DOWN THERE, ZUKO!

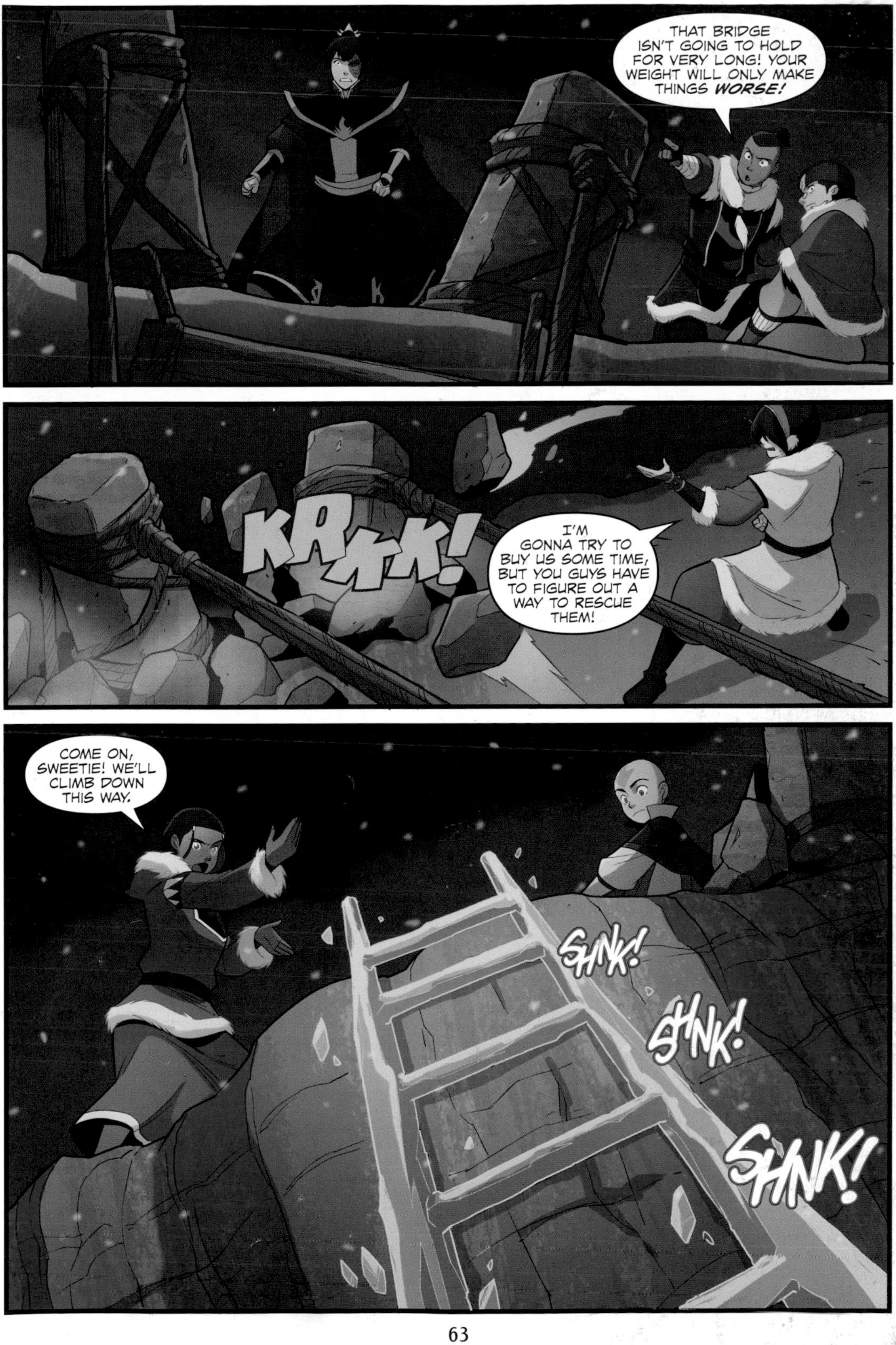
THAT BRIDGE ISN'T GOING TO HOLD FOR VERY LONG! YOUR WEIGHT WILL ONLY MAKE THINGS ***WORSE!***
KRKK!
I'M GONNA TRY TO BUY US SOME TIME, BUT YOU GUYS HAVE TO FIGURE OUT A WAY TO RESCUE THEM!
COME ON, SWEETIE! WE'LL CLIMB DOWN THIS WAY.
SHNK!
SHNK!
SHNK!

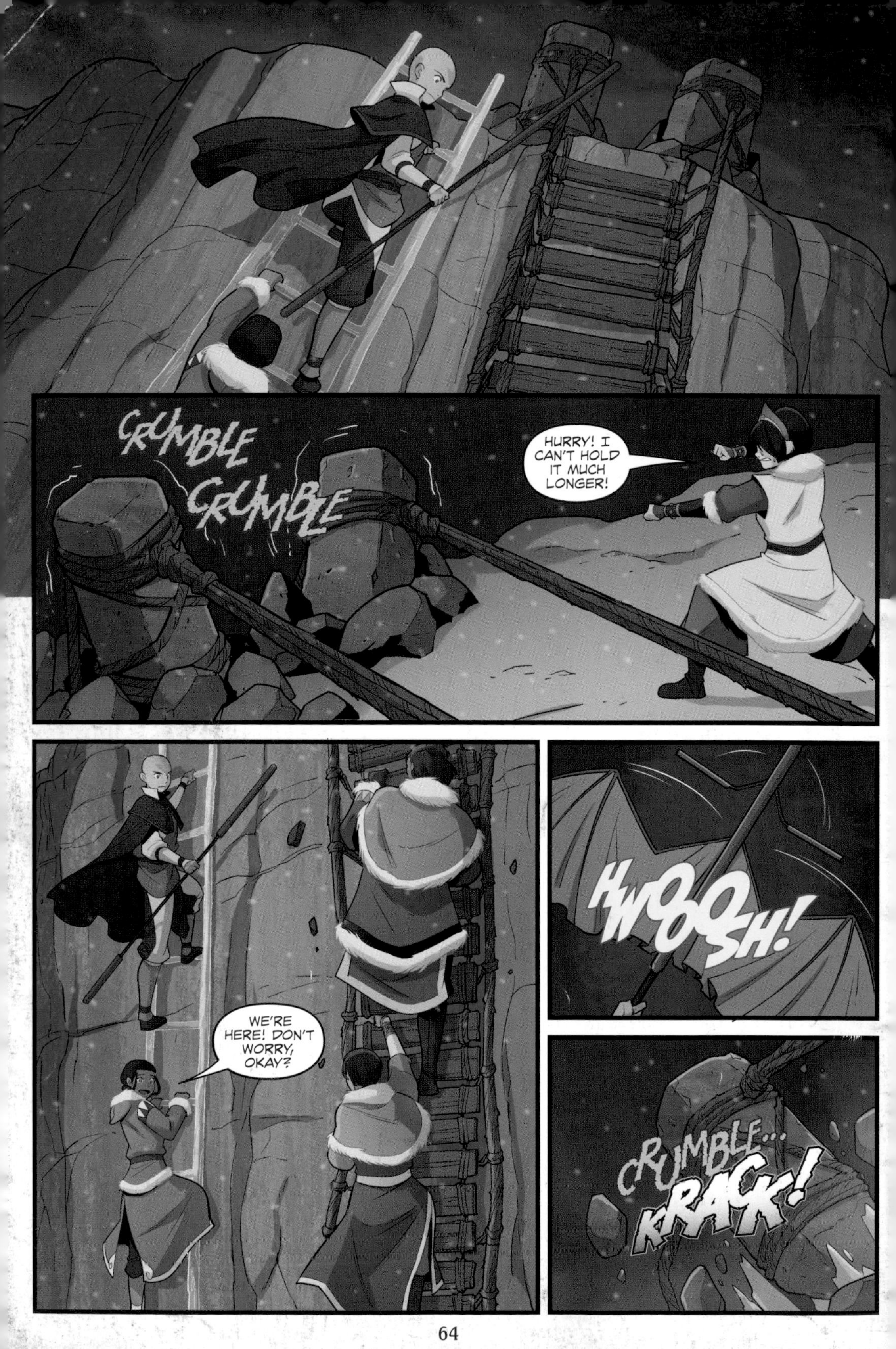
CRUMBLE
CRUMBLE
HURRY! I CAN'T HOLD IT MUCH LONGER!
WE'RE HERE! DON'T WORRY, OKAY?
HWOOOSH!
CRUMBLE...
KRACK!

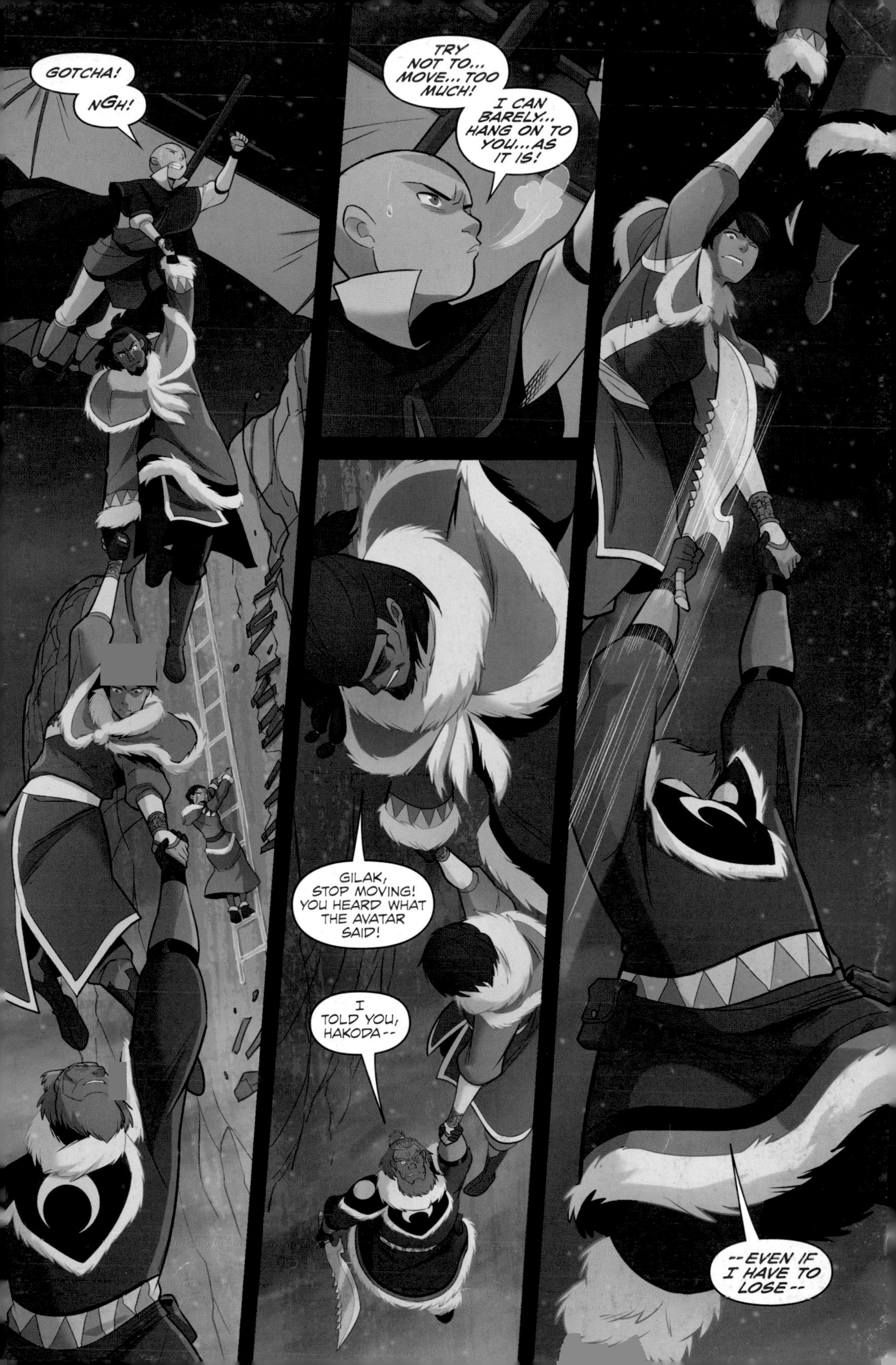
GOTCHA!
NGH!
TRY NOT TO... MOVE... TOO MUCH!
I CAN BARELY... HANG ON TO YOU... AS IT IS!
GILAK, STOP MOVING! YOU HEARD WHAT THE AVATAR SAID!
I TOLD YOU, HAKODA--
--EVEN IF I HAVE TO LOSE--

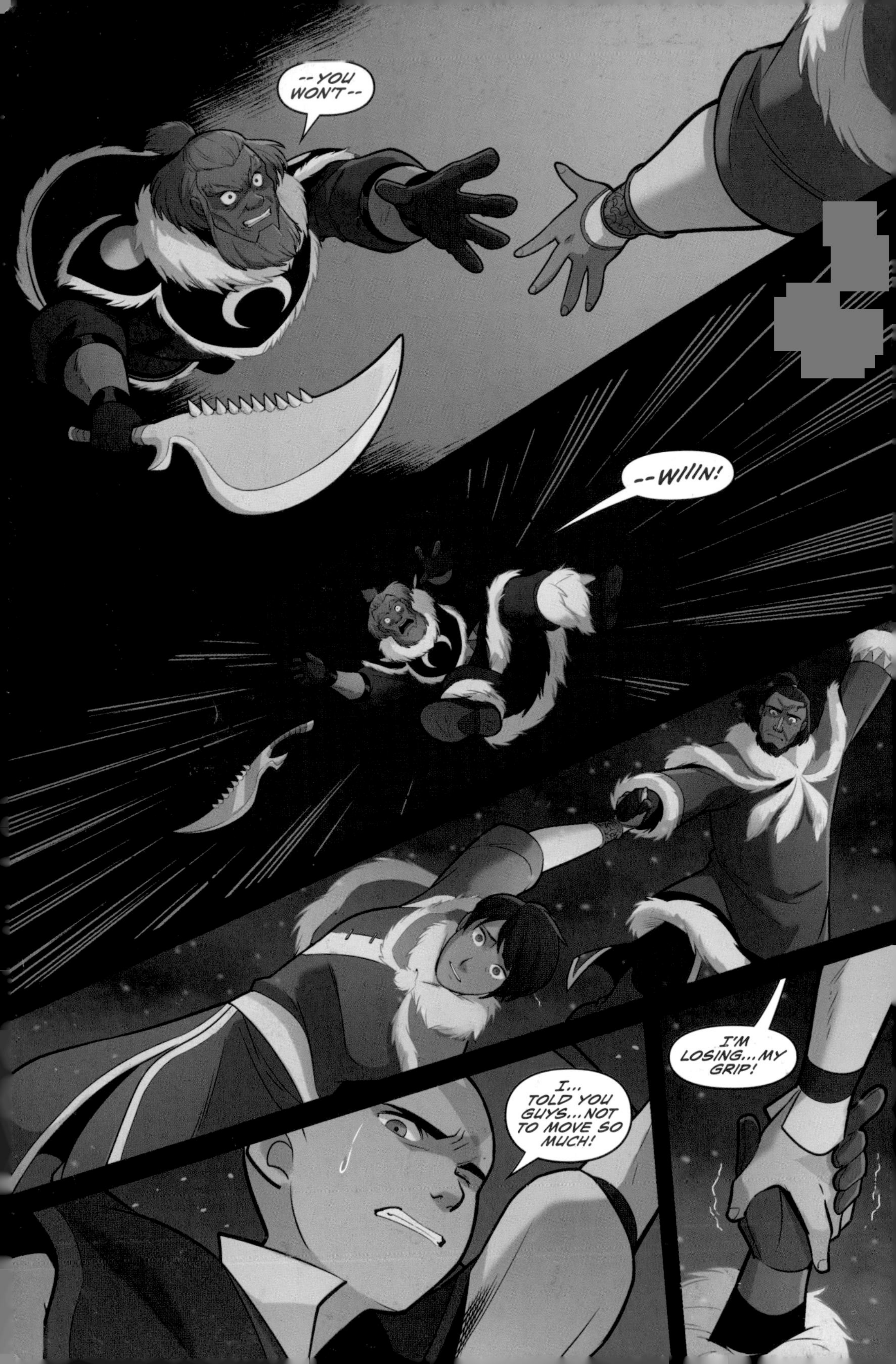
--YOU WON'T--
--WIIIN!
I'M LOSING...MY GRIP!
I... TOLD YOU GUYS...NOT TO MOVE SO MUCH!

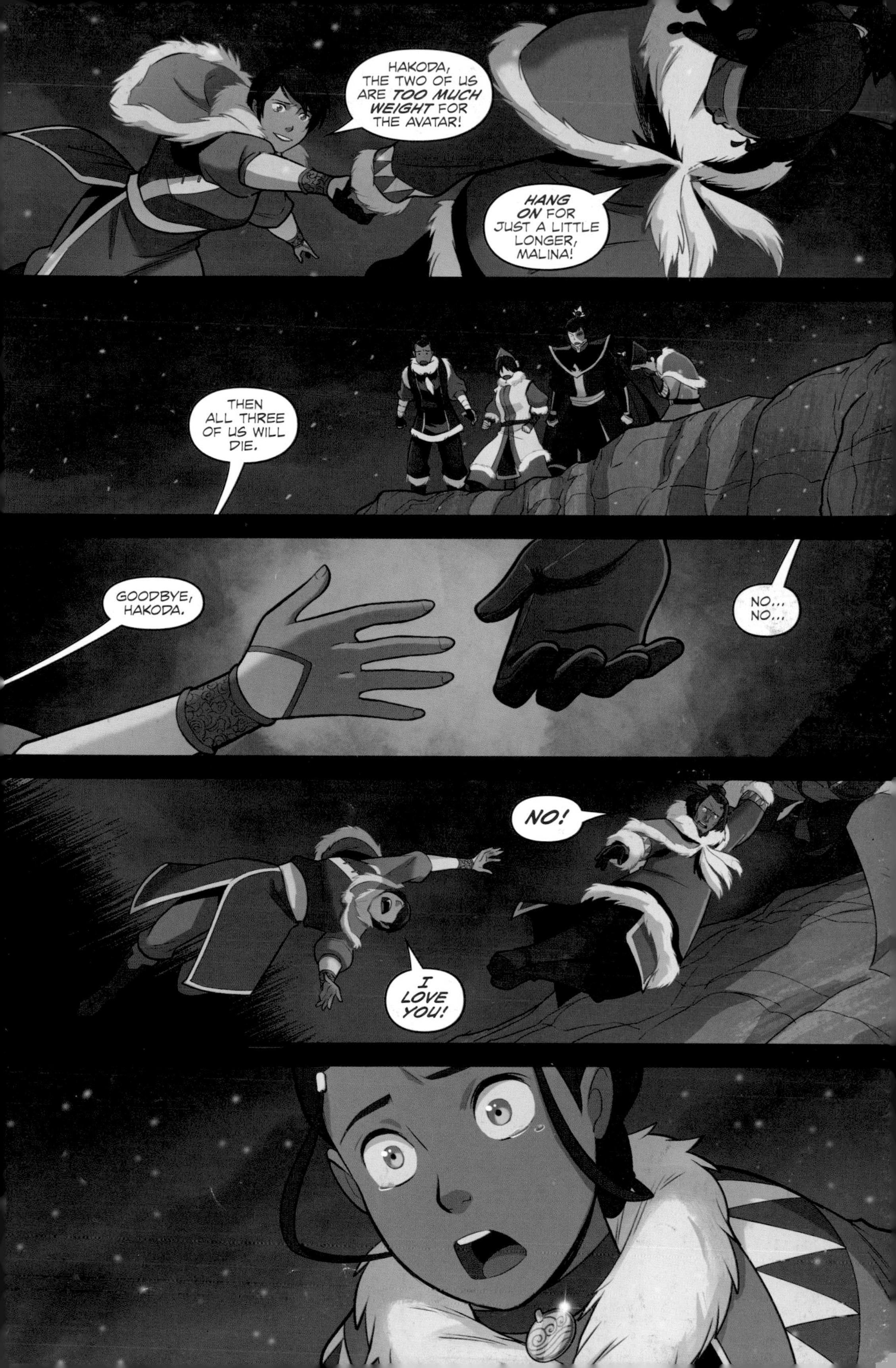
HAKODA, THE TWO OF US ARE **TOO MUCH WEIGHT** FOR THE AVATAR!
HANG ON FOR JUST A LITTLE LONGER, MALINA!
THEN ALL THREE OF US WILL DIE.
GOODBYE, HAKODA.
NO... NO...
NO!
I LOVE YOU!

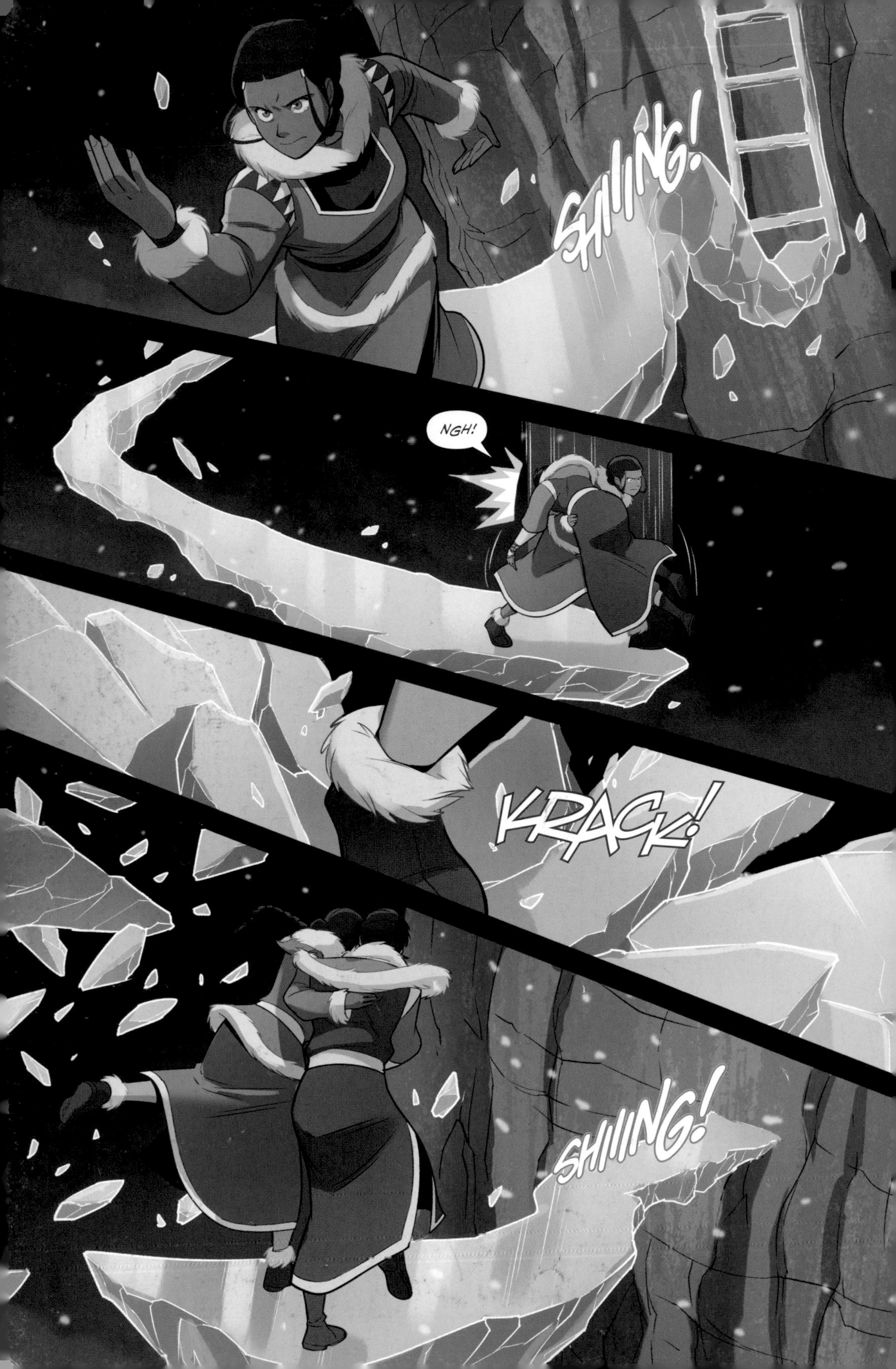
SHIIING!
NGH!
KRACK!
SHIIING!

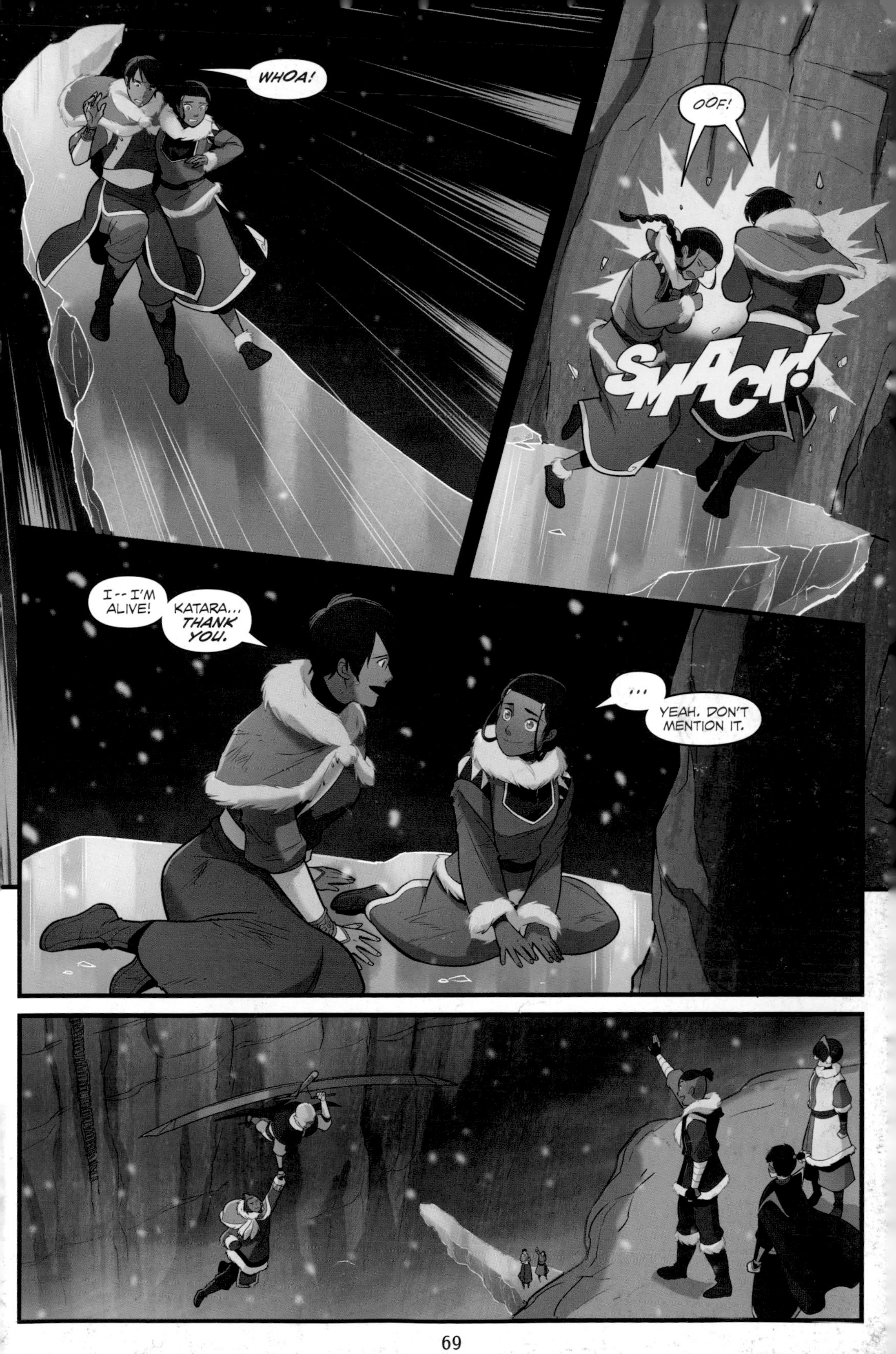
WHOA!
OOF!
SMACK!
I -- I'M ALIVE!
KATARA... THANK YOU.
...
YEAH. DON'T MENTION IT.

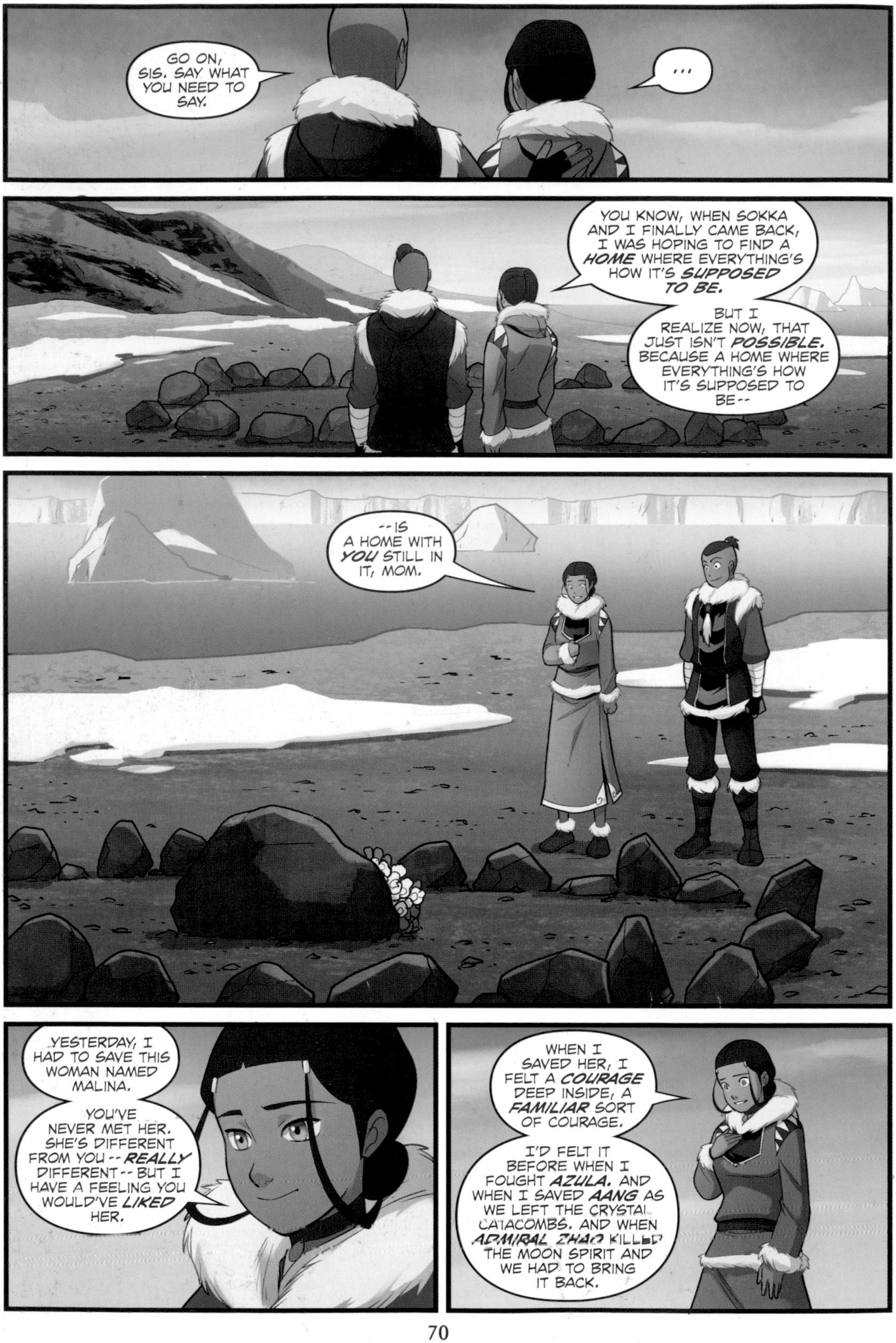
GO ON, SIS. SAY WHAT YOU NEED TO SAY.
...
YOU KNOW, WHEN SOKKA AND I FINALLY CAME BACK, I WAS HOPING TO FIND A HOME WHERE EVERYTHING'S HOW IT'S SUPPOSED TO BE.
BUT I REALIZE NOW, THAT JUST ISN'T POSSIBLE. BECAUSE A HOME WHERE EVERYTHING'S HOW IT'S SUPPOSED TO BE--
--IS A HOME WITH YOU STILL IN IT, MOM.
YESTERDAY, I HAD TO SAVE THIS WOMAN NAMED MALINA.
YOU'VE NEVER MET HER. SHE'S DIFFERENT FROM YOU--REALLY DIFFERENT--BUT I HAVE A FEELING YOU WOULD'VE LIKED HER.
WHEN I SAVED HER, I FELT A COURAGE DEEP INSIDE, A FAMILIAR SORT OF COURAGE.
I'D FELT IT BEFORE WHEN I FOUGHT AZULA. AND WHEN I SAVED AANG AS WE LEFT THE CRYSTAL CATACOMBS. AND WHEN ADMIRAL ZHAO KILLED THE MOON SPIRIT AND WE HAD TO BRING IT BACK.

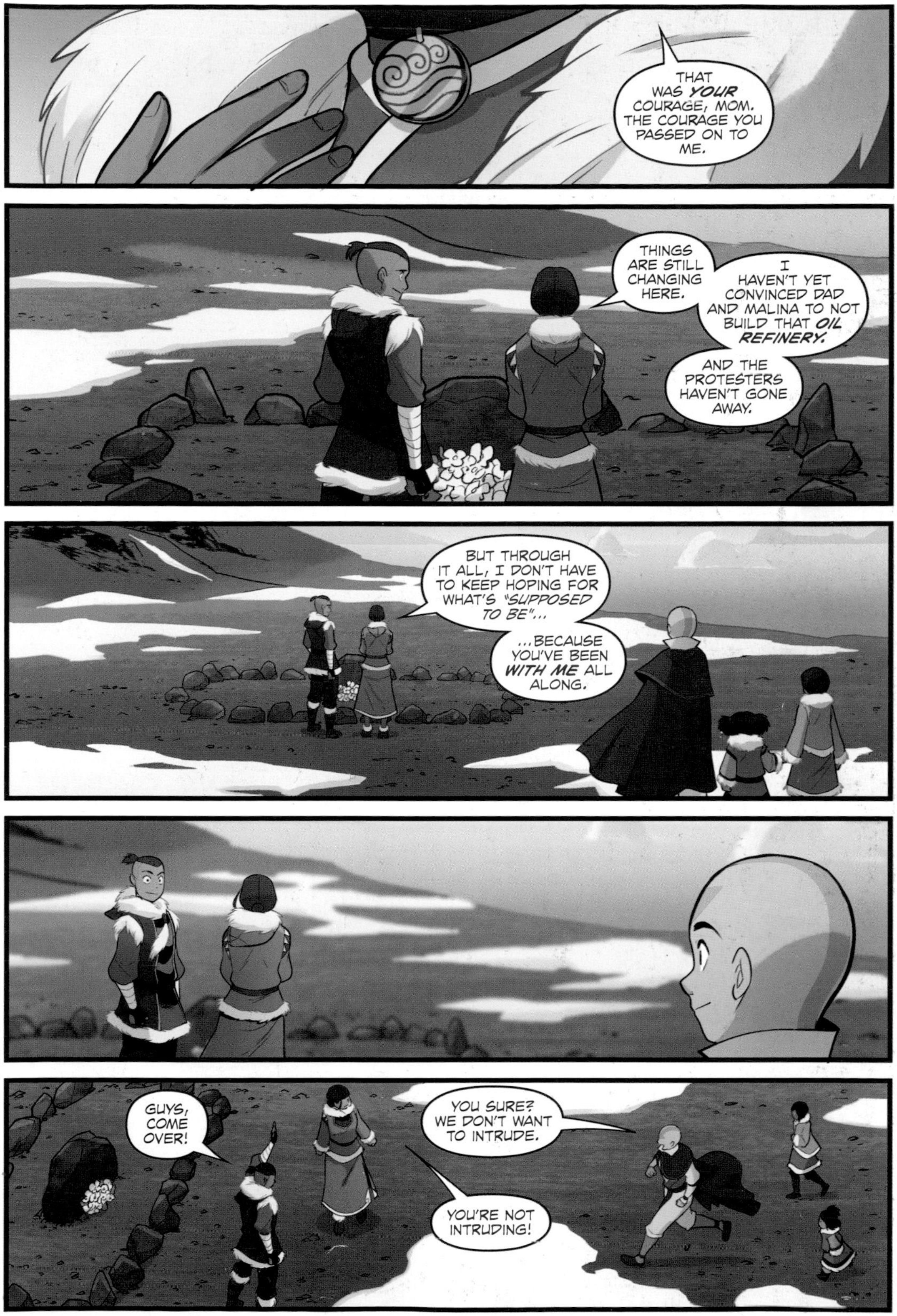
THAT WAS YOUR COURAGE, MOM. THE COURAGE YOU PASSED ON TO ME.
THINGS ARE STILL CHANGING HERE.
I HAVEN'T YET CONVINCED DAD AND MALINA TO NOT BUILD THAT OIL REFINERY.
AND THE PROTESTERS HAVEN'T GONE AWAY.
BUT THROUGH IT ALL, I DON'T HAVE TO KEEP HOPING FOR WHAT'S "SUPPOSED TO BE"...
...BECAUSE YOU'VE BEEN WITH ME ALL ALONG.
GUYS, COME OVER!
YOU SURE? WE DON'T WANT TO INTRUDE.
YOU'RE NOT INTRUDING!

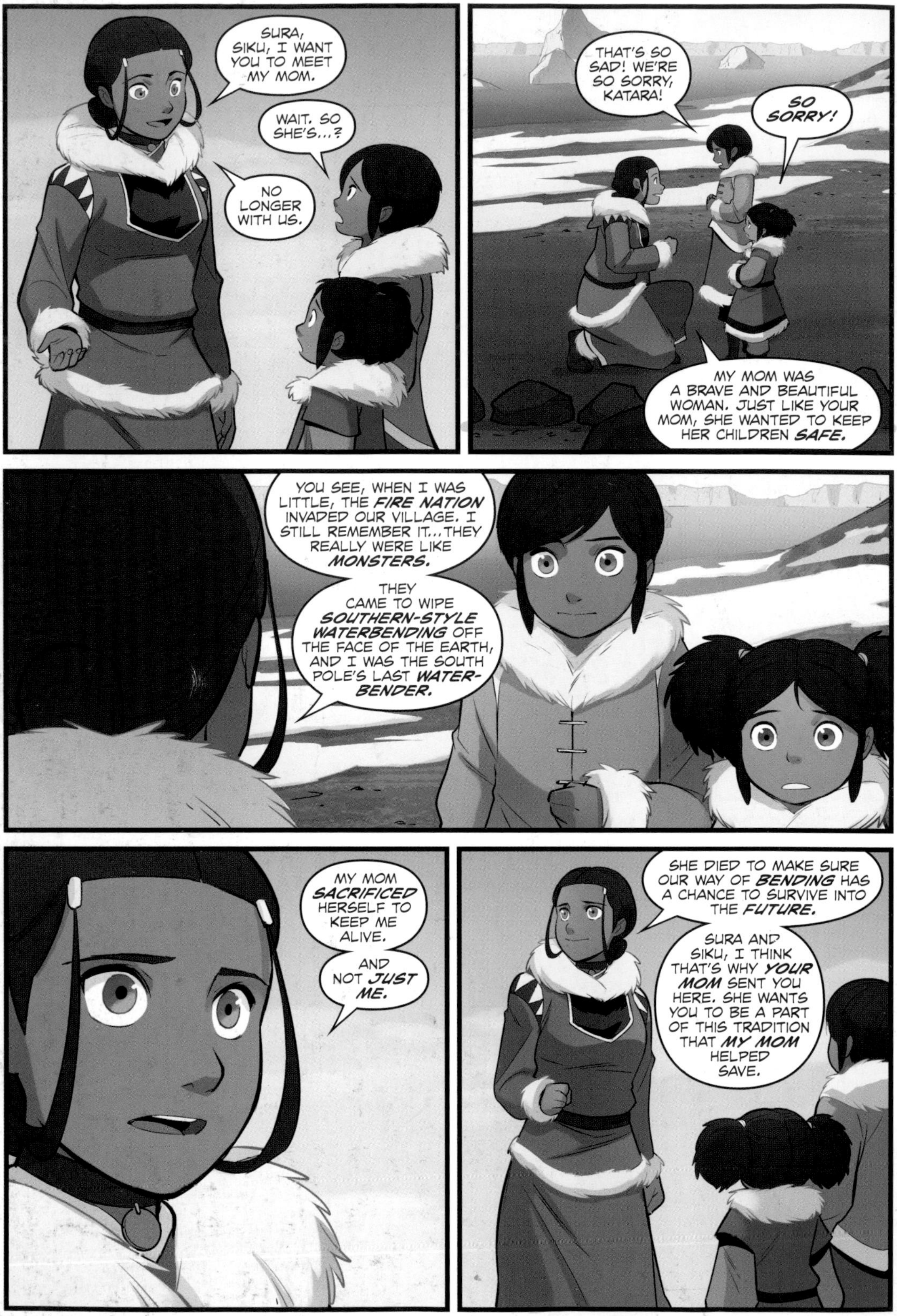
SURA, SIKU, I WANT YOU TO MEET MY MOM.
WAIT. SO SHE'S...?
NO LONGER WITH US.
THAT'S SO SAD! WE'RE SO SORRY, KATARA!
SO SORRY!
MY MOM WAS A BRAVE AND BEAUTIFUL WOMAN. JUST LIKE YOUR MOM, SHE WANTED TO KEEP HER CHILDREN SAFE.
YOU SEE, WHEN I WAS LITTLE, THE FIRE NATION INVADED OUR VILLAGE. I STILL REMEMBER IT... THEY REALLY WERE LIKE MONSTERS.
THEY CAME TO WIPE SOUTHERN-STYLE WATERBENDING OFF THE FACE OF THE EARTH, AND I WAS THE SOUTH POLE'S LAST WATER-BENDER.
MY MOM SACRIFICED HERSELF TO KEEP ME ALIVE.
AND NOT JUST ME.
SHE DIED TO MAKE SURE OUR WAY OF BENDING HAS A CHANCE TO SURVIVE INTO THE FUTURE.
SURA AND SIKU, I THINK THAT'S WHY YOUR MOM SENT YOU HERE. SHE WANTS YOU TO BE A PART OF THIS TRADITION THAT MY MOM HELPED SAVE.

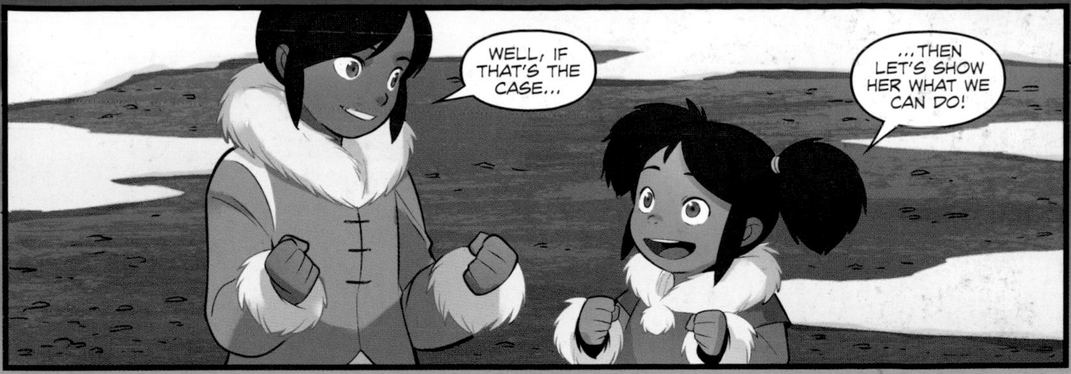
WELL, IF THAT'S THE CASE...
...THEN LET'S SHOW HER WHAT WE CAN DO!
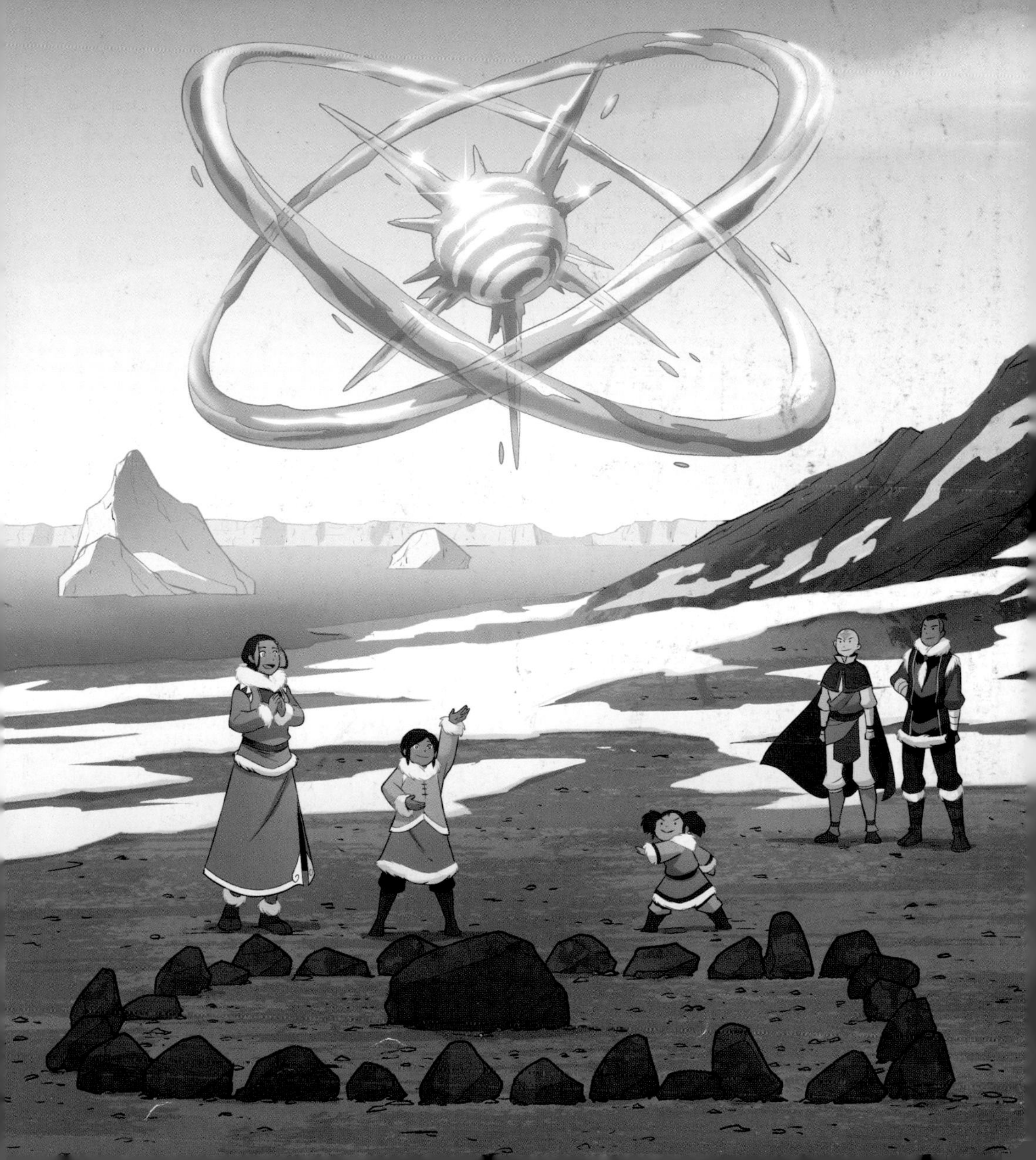

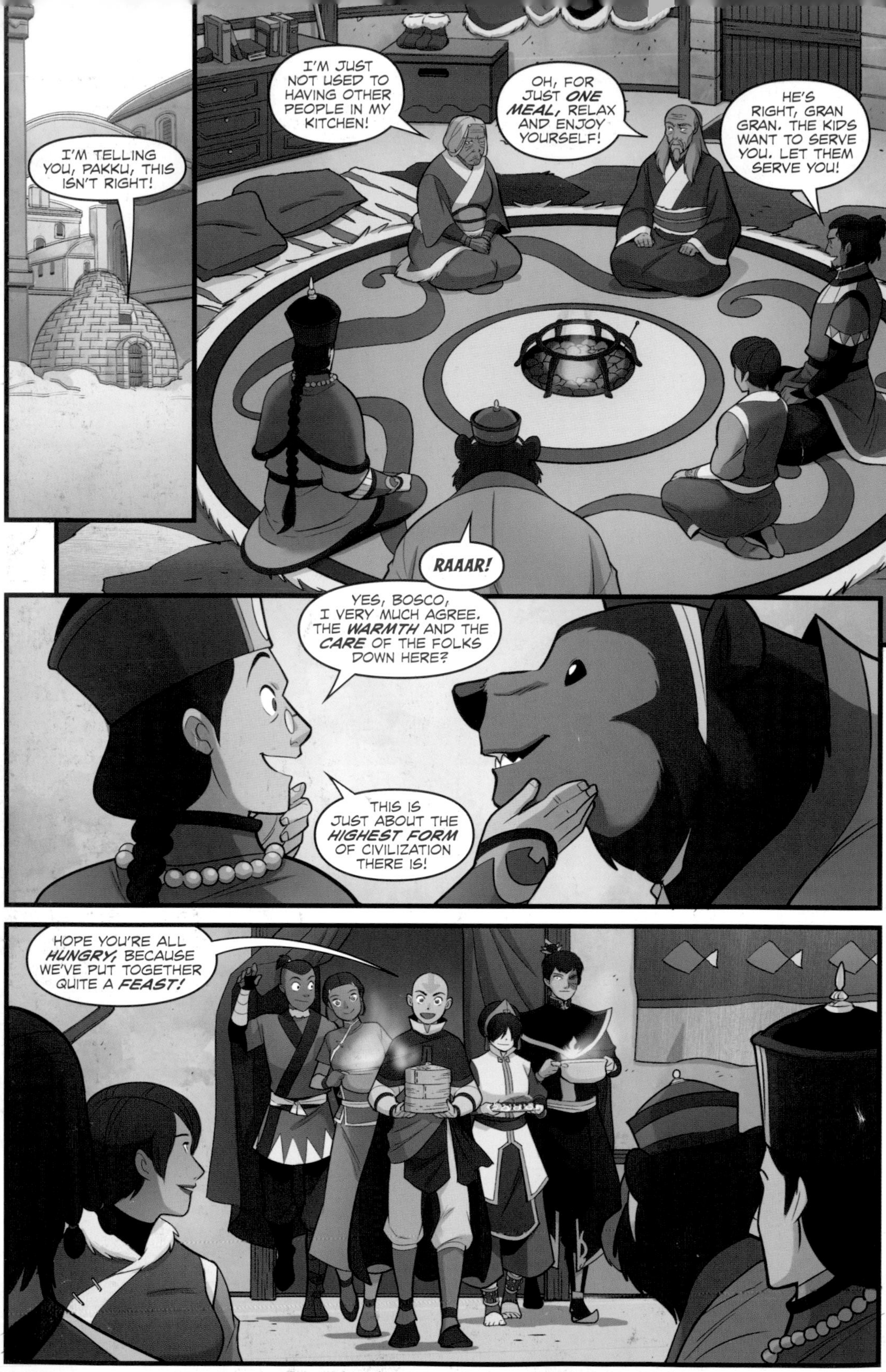
I'M TELLING YOU, PAKKU, THIS ISN'T RIGHT!
I'M JUST NOT USED TO HAVING OTHER PEOPLE IN MY KITCHEN!
OH, FOR JUST ONE MEAL, RELAX AND ENJOY YOURSELF!
HE'S RIGHT, GRAN GRAN. THE KIDS WANT TO SERVE YOU. LET THEM SERVE YOU!
RAAAR!
YES, BOSCO, I VERY MUCH AGREE. THE WARMTH AND THE CARE OF THE FOLKS DOWN HERE?
THIS IS JUST ABOUT THE HIGHEST FORM OF CIVILIZATION THERE IS!
HOPE YOU'RE ALL HUNGRY, BECAUSE WE'VE PUT TOGETHER QUITE A FEAST!

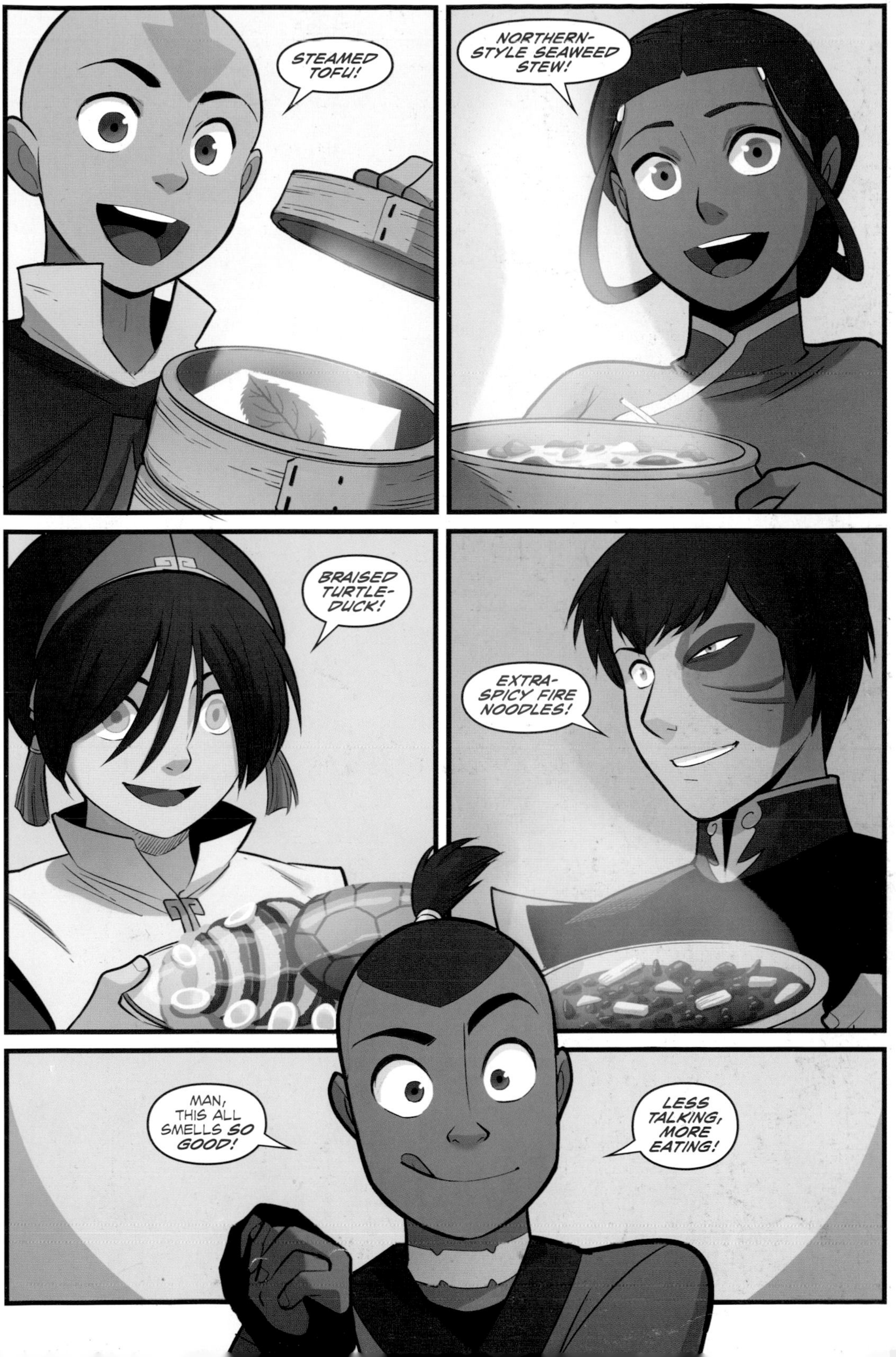
STEAMED TOFU!
NORTHERN-STYLE SEAWEED STEW!
BRAISED TURTLE-DUCK!
EXTRA-SPICY FIRE NOODLES!
MAN, THIS ALL SMELLS SO GOOD!
LESS TALKING, MORE EATING!

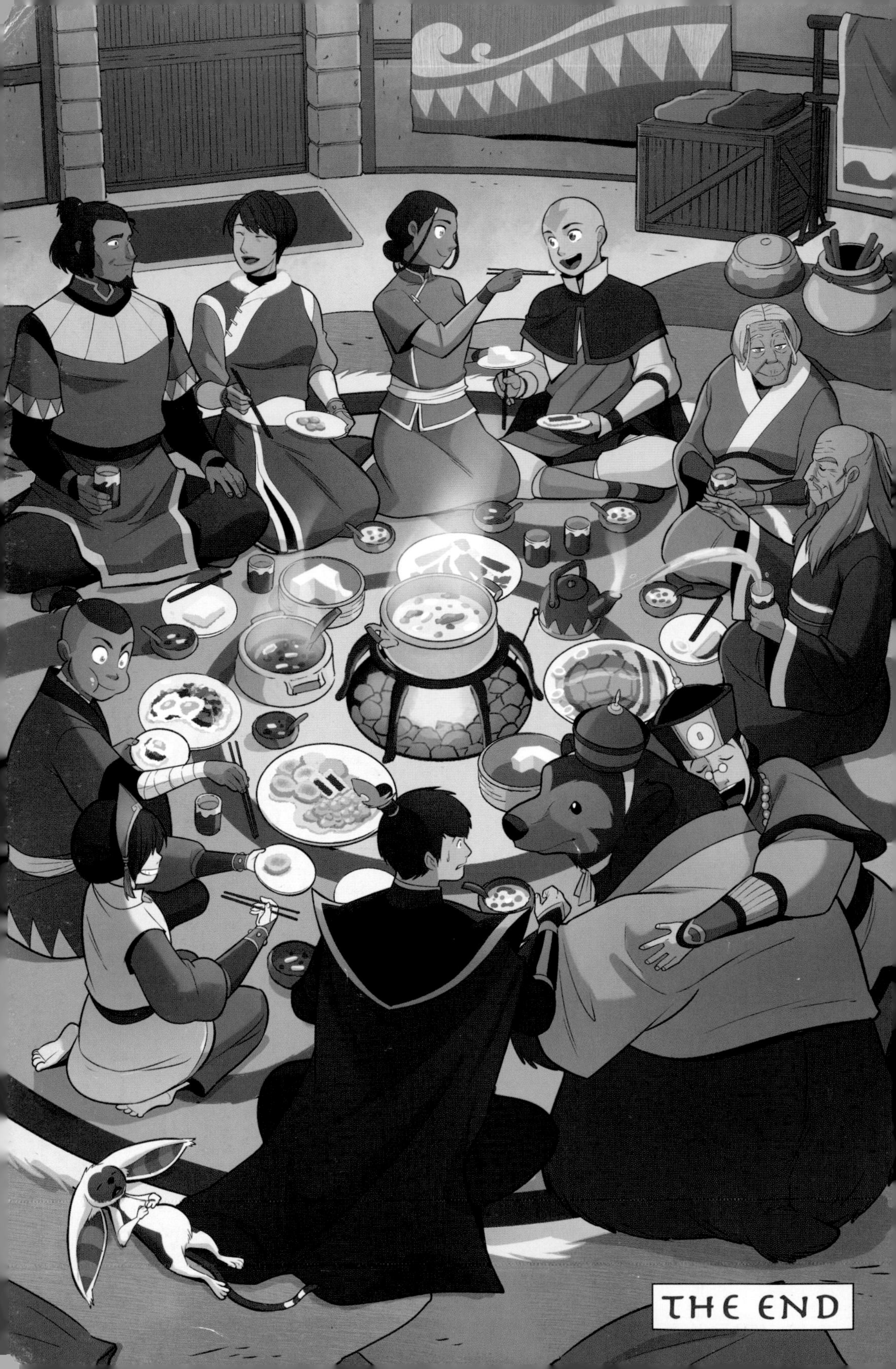
THE END

AVATAR
THE LAST AIRBENDER

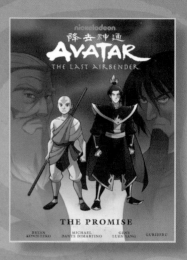